Duffy's World

"This book takes you through the life and times of an energetic, mischievous, and much loved canine companion. *Duffy's World* is chocked full of practical tips and good advice on dog ownership. Duffy's lessons in life are shared in short, entertaining, real-life stories from both the human and canine perspectives. What a lovely tribute to Duffy and his zest for life."

—**Sharon Nelson**, Founder, North American
Dog Agility Council (NADAC)

"My first impression in reading your novel was remembering the bond I had with Chance. He was my first Aussie, my first show dog, my first agility dog, my first stockdog, but much more than all that he was my heart dog. I learned a lot from Chance in all the years we were together. I am enjoying the memories again while reading your novel."

—**Nancy Resetar**, Chances' R Australian Shepherds
Owner of 2006 Crufts Best in Show winner, Caitland Isle Take a Chance

"Dog owners always want to know what their K-9 companions are thinking. Faith McCune tries to bring that perspective to life in *Duffy's World, Seeing the World through a Dog's Eyes*. We get a chance to follow Faith and Duffy while they explore everything from puppyhood, vet trips, and play time to fireworks, territory boundaries, and holidays. Faith touches on topics that first time Aussie owners may not think about and tries to help prospective Aussie owners learn from her encounters. She incorporates tips throughout the book that cover an assortment of topics. Anyone interested in Aussies should read this book and next time you are sitting on the back patio with Fido, just look into those eyes and see if you can figure out what is going through that head."

—**Ray Fryar**, Manager, Australian Shepherd Club of America

"Dogs are such an important part of my life. My job allows me to be around animals everyday, especially dogs, so I get to interact with so many. Duffy's story touched my heart as a dog lover. I thoroughly enjoyed your insight into Duffy's thoughts and enjoyed his many adventures. One of the reasons I enjoy the companionship of my canines so much is that they have so much to give and teach us as humans. Your book made me laugh and made me cry."

—**Julie Hanson**, Registered Veterinary Technician,
Center Veterinary Clinic, San Diego

Duffy's World

Seeing the World through a Dog's Eyes

Faith McCune

NEW YORK

Duffy's World
Seeing the World through a Dog's Eyes

Published in New York, New York, by Morgan James Publishing. Morgan James and The Entrepreneurial Publisher are trademarks of Morgan James, LLC. www.MorganJamesPublishing.com

The Morgan James Speakers Group can bring authors to your live event. For more information or to book an event visit The Morgan James Speakers Group at www.TheMorganJamesSpeakersGroup.com.

FREE eBook edition for your existing eReader with purchase

PRINT NAME ABOVE

For more information, instructions, restrictions, and to register your copy, go to **www.bitlit.ca/readers/register** or use your QR Reader to scan the barcode:

ISBN 978-1-61448-719-7 paperback
ISBN 978-1-61448-855-2 hard cover
ISBN 978-1-61448-720-3 eBook
ISBN 978-1-61448-721-0 audio
Library of Congress Control Number:
2013945568

Cover Design by:
Chris Treccani
www.3dogdesign.net

Interior Design by:
Bonnie Bushman
bonnie@caboodlegraphics.com

In an effort to support local communities, raise awareness and funds, Morgan James Publishing donates a percentage of all book sales for the life of each book to Habitat for Humanity Peninsula and Greater Williamsburg.

Get involved today, visit
www.MorganJamesBuilds.com.

Habitat for Humanity®
Peninsula and
Greater Williamsburg
Building Partner

Duffy's World is based on a true story. The dogs, names, places, and lessons learned are very real. However, Duffy's thoughts were fictionally dramatized, and creative license was taken regarding the timeline of a few events.

Contents

Introduction

From the moment I saw him, Duffy stole my heart. It was love at first sight! I didn't know anything about his breed so I had no idea what to expect from an Australian Shepherd. All I wanted was a dog who liked to cuddle; a dog who would be a happy member of a rather sedate family.

I soon learned that Australian Shepherds are *not* lap dogs, cuddlers (with occasional exceptions), or sedate. Duffy's brain worked as fast as his paws and teeth. Throughout his nearly thirteen years as a member of our family, keeping him entertained and out of trouble were our top priorities.

Duffy learned the basics of potty training and inappropriate chewing easily. Once he slowed down enough to see what we wanted him to do, he reveled in his training. We marveled at how quickly he learned new skills. It only took one or two tries for him to figure out what we expected. His intelligence from an early age was remarkable. But each new experience brought its own challenges. As a puppy, his willful independence undermined our initial attempts at training. His belief that his way was the right way did not change. His over-the-top zest for life kept us guessing and, yes, constantly stressed. Since we were novices with the breed as well, our ignorance only added to the chaos.

Over time, he gave us the ride of our lives. What I didn't realize when I first laid eyes on Duffy was how much he would teach *me* about raising a dog.

Duffy's story is told, for the most part, from his perspective. My comments provide some clarity to the situation, but his unique point of view is what he expressed to me with his eyes, ears, and body language.

For those of us who've raised many dogs during our lives, we know there is "dog speak." We hear it every day. If you haven't experienced this yet, spend a moment observing your dog, or someone else's, for a few minutes. Once you "hear" that voice, you'll discover a unique form of communication that's rich without words.

The Beginning

My brothers, sisters, and I shared a cramped space until the flood came. It pushed us through a tight tunnel one by one. I tried to hang on when everybody went but couldn't. I was the last to go.

My first breath in my new world was shocking. Cold! The newness of it all made me cry out. I was wet too, but somebody warm pulled me close and licked me a lot. My mom! I got my first taste of real food too. Yum! I stayed soggy for a long time. Long.

I liked this place. My sisters and brothers did too. We had lots more space to move around, and the food was good. I couldn't see or hear anything yet, but I smelled my mom. She kept me close and licked me all the time. She loved me a lot. She didn't say so, but I knew I was special.

I smelled other things too but didn't know what they were. I had a hard time staying awake. Hunger woke me, but after I ate I fell asleep.

Soon I started hearing noises and seeing shadows moving around. My brothers and sisters were awake. Me too! We climbed on each other to get to the best spot by mom. I couldn't move around too far. I was still the smallest, but I was strong, so I ate good.

Mom called me "Uff-uff." My brothers and sisters too. I was her favorite, though. I could tell. I'd cry and she'd come get me right away. My sisters and brothers didn't move around much yet, but I liked to smell everything. So many new things to explore! Still can't stand up too long. Shaky. But I try. Try.

I can finally walk now. My paws aren't too strong yet. I met mom's humans. They liked to hold us. My brothers and sisters liked it but not me. It reminded me of our flooded home. Too tight! They squeezed harder when I fought so I fought some more. Mom said I should be a good puppy like the others and pay attention to her so I don't get in Trouble. Don't know who Trouble is. Might be a bad human. I watched for him and tried to be good. Mom worried about me. She said, "Independence is not always a good thing."

We all liked to play with each other now that we're bigger. My sisters played nice, but my brothers jumped on me and bit me all the time. I didn't like that, so I fought and bit them back. I grew little teeth so I let them know who was boss. Sometimes they'd gang up on me. My brothers didn't like me much. Mom said I'm bossy, but I just liked to play and find new stuff, though I didn't mind a good fight either. I'm still the smallest, but I'm tough. When we played, my brothers quit if I fought too hard.

 Chapter 1

My New Home

Choices

"I want a dog!" I declared.

We didn't have a dog for five years and I missed the companionship and love of a warm, furry canine. I scoured mall pet stores for months admiring and often playing with the puppies on display, longing for one of my own. Sometimes I'd linger with one or two, but didn't want to pay hundreds of dollars for a pet store puppy. Many of them came from puppy mills and weren't healthy. After another discouraging visit, my husband, Bernard, suggested, "Why don't you check the newspaper? A family-raised puppy might be in better condition and they might not want as much for a dog."

Serendipity! The first ad in the newspaper the next day announced a litter of Australian Shepherd puppies ready for adoption. They wanted fifty dollars for their little Aussies. I'd never seen an Australian Shepherd at the mall stores before, but it certainly wouldn't hurt to look. "What a deal!" I exclaimed.

When I showed him the ad, Bernard said, "Why don't you go take a look? But just look!"

I called the number in the ad and arranged a meeting that day to see their female puppy. They lived thirty minutes away, so I drove to their home, without Bernard, to look at her.

The entire family met me at the door. The woman I spoke to earlier invited me in and brought me the little female we'd discussed. I wasn't captivated by this tiny puppy, even though she appeared docile and sweet. I was disappointed and started to leave.

Before I reached the door, I heard more puppies playing outside and asked to see them. The woman said, "They're all males and more, ah, assertive than the female."

When she opened the patio door, four puppies tumbled in from the yard and bounced at our feet. The littlest one scurried around, trying to find an opening from the back of the pack. It looked as though he was saying, "Pick me! Pick me!" He was gorgeous.

When he finally broke through, this wild child flew into the house and into my heart. I couldn't resist him, even though he dashed off before I could get a good look at him. I laughed. He was such a rascal! It took all four of the family to catch him, but I finally held him in my arms and knew instantly he was the one for me! "Oh, he's so beautiful," I gushed. I was unprepared to bring a puppy home, but I couldn't leave without him. My excitement overshadowed my common sense. I forgot Bernard's plea to "just look." My emotions clouded my perspective. I didn't stop to analyze the consequences of my actions.

I remember it a little differently. One day a new human came to look at my sister. I had two sisters before, but another human took one and she never came home again. This human didn't like my leftover sister. Too homely and not as smart as me. Or cute.

She asked to see us boys. My mom's human opened the yard door. My brothers pushed me back so I couldn't get in. "Let me in! Me first!" I saw my chance. I ran in and slipped on the kitchen floor. I hit mom's water bowl. Splash! Up went the food bowl. Kibble flew all around. Yum! This was good stuff, but I was too busy to eat. Everybody chased me. I ran down the hall, but the boy human caught me. I didn't like being held. I fought hard but couldn't get away. They all laughed. My humans laughed all the time, even when they said they wanted to kill me.

The new human said I was the cutest puppy she ever saw. I had to admit she was right. She grabbed me too and held tight so I couldn't get away. I kicked and fought, but I was trapped. "Let go! Let me down! I want to play!"

Mom's humans told her I'm an Australian Shepherd and the runt of the litter. I think runt meant small, but I wasn't sure. So much to learn. I think the new human's smarter than mom's humans. She called me a puppy.

What's an Australian Shepherd anyway? Mom said I'm an Aussie. I guessed that meant bossy. Mom called me that a lot. I don't know why. I made humans laugh all the time. Why are they always grabbing me? I played better than my brothers and sisters, but every time the humans chased me they said they're going to kill me! I ran real fast then.

I told the family, "I want this one!" I looked very tenderly at my fidgety pup and said, "I'm your mama! I'm going to love you *forever!*"

Mom's humans put me in a box and stuffed me in a car with this stranger. My mom whimpered, "Don't take my boy!" but all the humans smiled and laughed. Everybody was happy but me. And mom. What happened? I'm afraid. "Mom! Help! Is this Trouble? Where am I going? Is this human going to kill me? Eat me? Mom! M-o-m!" I cried and cried, but she didn't come get me this time. I was kidnapped like my sister. I never saw my mom again.

I sat in the box crying for a long time. Long time. Long! I wanted my mom! I wasn't a happy boy anymore. I was afraid I wouldn't find my way back and my mom needed me. I know. I heard her whine when I left. That made me cry more. Rooo! This human called Mama said I have a cute howl, but I wasn't feeling too cute anymore.

TIPS:

Ease into the adoption process. Your puppy doesn't know you yet and may be unprepared for the change. Be gentle and calm when you remove a puppy from his mother and/or current home. Let him accept you first. Comfort and reassure him on his first journey to his new home.

Be sure the puppy's temperament is appropriate for your lifestyle.

Homecoming

My little pup managed to stay in the box during our drive home and serenaded me with little howls. His lips formed a perfect oval as he lifted his head and wailed his mournful cries. It was so endearing that I wanted to pick him up and hold him, but couldn't because I had to drive.

As I pulled into our driveway, I could hardly contain my excitement. "Daddy will be so surprised," I told my pup.

> There's another human? Is this one Trouble? I tried to be brave, but I couldn't.

I burst through the door and said, "Guess what? I got my puppy!"

The expression on Bernard's face was not what I'd hoped to see. "Hon, I thought you were going to just look! It really isn't a good time to have a dog."

I was stunned. All along, I thought a dog was in both our plans. Bernard's displeasure was apparent. I'd come home with a new pet, but he didn't have any input. He never dreamed I'd impulsively bring a puppy home after all those unsuccessful visits to the pet stores. It was so out of character for me! He also worried about our semi-feral cat's reaction to this tiny intruder. I hadn't even thought about our cat.

 TIPS:

The entire family should agree that the timing is right before getting a dog.

The puppy will be everyone's responsibility. Caring for the dog should be shared by the entire family.

When I got to my new home, I met Daddy. He's a big dude! Bigger than my mom's humans. Big! Way big! I was really scared. My mom told me about Trouble. I think I just met him, even though his name is Daddy. He didn't like me. I could feel how mad he was. He's going to kill me for sure. Good-bye. Life is short. Way short! I cried some more.

Mama gave me chicken. I tried not to eat, but all my crying made me hungry. I ate as much as she gave me. Yum! I forgot my fears for the moment. Food tends to do that. Mama picked me up and held me. I was too tired to struggle.

"Look how cute he is! So cuddly and sweet. We're your new parents and we'll love you *forever!*" I held and stroked him until he fell asleep. I loved this little puppy already. Bernard saw how adorable he was and reluctantly agreed to let him stay if he got along with our cat.

I fell asleep! Embarrassing! How am I going to escape and find my way home if I fall asleep? At least I wasn't dead yet so I wasn't scared anymore. That's when I met my stupid sister. Back then I thought my sister was stupid because she didn't speak "dog." Everybody I knew spoke "dog" except humans. It took a while for me to understand her, but she wasn't stupid. She was smart at what she knew. She just wasn't dog smart. Like me. Mama said her name was Jingles and she's a cat. I never met a cat before. She smelled funny too. Stinky. Not like my family or humans. She rubbed her head all over me. She made me feel safe, just like with mom, even though Jingles didn't smell so good.

The rest of the day passed quickly after I returned home. Jingles' reception to our new family member eased Bernard's concerns. "Whew, we dodged *that* bullet! She could've scratched his eyes out or had him for lunch! That was pretty cute how she rubbed her scent all over him," Bernard said.

"Yes," I agreed. I was thinking the same thing, thankful that Jingles accepted our pup.

TIPS:

Never be impulsive when adopting a dog. If the dog will be a family pet, then the family needs to choose him together.

Remember the other animals in your home before you bring in a new pet. Some relationships won't work. Introduce your pets to each other, in a neutral environment if possible, before you make a final decision.

The Pet Store

We needed to get supplies and food for our new pup. So into the car we went with the squirmy little tyke in tow. He was all claws and teeth, but I managed to keep from dropping him. He would've made a run for it and I'd never catch him.

We bought a huge bag of food and a few toys. The clerk suggested we stock up on training and cleaning supplies as well. Our pup was almost eight weeks old and full of untamed mischief and boundless energy. She said we needed to redirect that energy so he doesn't destroy our home. Good idea! Now, how do we do that?

Mama and Daddy stuffed me in the car again. I was afraid! The car was not my friend. It just kept humming when I was crying for help. I won't ever know how to get back to my mom if we kept moving! I tried to climb out of Mama's lap and scratched her. She yowled but didn't bite me. My mom did a couple times. Hard. She said "grrrrrrrrr" a lot too. Mostly to me. Maybe because she chased me more than my brothers and sisters.

We stopped at a place called Pet Store. Mama said it's "Petco where the pets go!" Daddy laughed, but I didn't see any pets. What's a Pet? I wondered. Don't know Pet. Just dog, puppy, and now cat. It took me a while to learn *I* was a pet. No wonder humans are confused all the time! They can't seem to get our names straight.

Mama picked up a big noisy bag that smelled like food. She called it kibble. There are so many new words to learn! Pet Store, now Kibble. Kibble smelled like the chicken I had, but it sounded like my mom's dinner. I liked chicken. It's my favorite! I sniffed the bag. Mama understood what I said because she got a big bag. I thought kibbles were alive! Kibbles made a lot of noise. They rolled down one side, and then the other when Mama held the bag. "I want to see! Can they come out and play?" When Daddy took the bag, they stayed quiet. Afraid of the big dude. He *must* be Trouble.

Mama got a couple toys and something called Wee-Wee Pads. She said they were for me. Didn't know what that was either, but I liked stuff if it's for me. A lot. Daddy got a big bottle of Nature's Miracle to drink. He must've been real thirsty. The "Petco where the pets go" human called the bottle "Thank Heaven." It must taste good because Daddy was happy to get it.

I found out later the bottle wasn't for him. It was to water the house grass. Only Daddy called it a carpet. Humans make simple things so confusing. Everybody got treats that day except for Jingles.

When we came home, I saw my first ball and a toy on a string. We played in the yard for a long time. Long. I ran and played until I couldn't play anymore. I heard Mama say, "Ten minutes is a lot for a little boy." Who's Ten Minutes? Never met Ten Minutes, but I hoped he wouldn't steal my toys when I got tired and fell asleep again. My toys! Mine!

After a quick dinner, we let him play with his new toys and explore the yard again. Spending a couple of hours with a new puppy was exhausting. He napped between romps, but he'd jump up again ready for more when he heard the slightest sound from us. We braced ourselves for a very long evening! Then it was time to put our little boy to bed.

We still only had the cardboard box to confine him so we lined it with a Wee-Wee Pad we got at the store and a soft towel to keep him warm. When we put him in his makeshift bed, he refused to settle down. He scratched at the box and cried incessantly for the next two nights until he finally adapted to our routine. We were completely sleep deprived by then.

I didn't sleep too good my first night. I missed my mom. Yes, even my brothers and leftover sister. Well, maybe…not. I got stuck in the box again and I cried to get out. Mama put a soft blanket on me and patted my head a couple times, but she didn't tuck me in to keep me warm like my mom. Jingles didn't stay either. That's okay. Stinky.

I finally fell asleep all alone. I felt sorry for myself. All alone. Scary. Just me and my Wee-Wee Pad in the box. And my little blanket. Sad. Nobody cared. "I want my mom! Rooo!"

I wondered if my mom missed me like I missed her. I didn't know what to expect now that I didn't have my mom to help me. My perfect life was over. My mom tried to teach me, but I didn't pay attention. I thought she would always be there when I needed her. I didn't listen like my brothers and sisters. I was too busy exploring or playing by myself. Independent. I liked it when my mom called me that. Sounded important. I'm not so sure anymore.

I was afraid of Mama and Daddy even though they were nice to me. I didn't know them. Would they kill me, eat me, throw me away, or put me in the box for good if I didn't do what they wanted? So many fears.

🐾 TIPS:

Buy food, cleaning supplies, and toys before you bring your puppy home. Include a little collar and leash on your shopping list.

Get an appropriate-sized crate for your puppy. It is not inhumane to crate your puppy for short periods while you're away or need a time-out. It's also a secure place for him to eat and sleep. This will soon become his safe haven, even though he may not seem to like it at first.

Expect the first few nights to be an adjustment for your puppy. Plan to take time off from work. You'll need the rest.

When I woke up the next morning, I learned that a Wee-Wee Pad had a purpose other than keeping my paws warm. Mama called my paws "foofies." Every puppy knows they're paws. She treats me like a baby. Embarrassing!

She tried to get me to potty on the Wee-Wee Pad at first, but it smelled funny. I put my front paws on it and peed on the house grass. Daddy called it a carpet. The Car had a Pet? I don't get it. Mama wasn't happy, but I thought I was pretty smart. She turned me around real quick. Whoa! Dizzy! Oh, no! I peed on my Wee-Wee Pad by mistake. She said I was a good boy so she wasn't mad. Safe! Daddy opened the bottle of "Thank Heaven for Nature's Miracle" to give the house grass a drink. Daddy wasn't too mad either so I guess he won't eat me. Not going back in the box either. Uh-uh. The next time I peed where Mama wanted and got a treat! Yum!

Hmmm. I get it now! I got cookies when I did what Mama wanted! I never peed on the house grass again. Not even on the Car Pet. Scary! I didn't like the car. I knew by then the car was Trouble. The car growled at me all the time.

 TIPS:

Be consistent when you teach your puppy new skills, especially potty training. Your puppy won't tell you when he needs to relieve himself.

Be proactive. Take him out every two or three hours, day or night, even if he doesn't have to go, to reinforce what you are trying to teach him. If that isn't possible, line his crate, or a designated box, with training pads.

Chapter 2

Puppy Training

The Doggie Door

We taught our pup to use the doggie door. We installed one years ago and it allowed Jingles to come and go as she pleased. We wanted our new pup to learn to use the door too. He was afraid at first, but the treats he received with every repetition encouraged him to continue practicing. We were thrilled he learned so fast!

Mama and Daddy said, "Let's teach him to use the doggie door." I didn't see any doggies. Just a wall in front of me. They wanted to squash me. Not going there. Uh-uh.

Mama stuffed me in the wall anyway and a hole appeared. The first time she did that I fought hard. I had to protect myself from these crazy humans! I pushed with my paws and saw the yard and Daddy on the other side. "Wow!" I thought. "How did he do that? Did Mama push him in the wall too?" When I went out, he grabbed me and stuffed me back in. Then Mama pushed me back out. I don't get it. I didn't know where they wanted me to go! So confused. Am I in or am I out? They made a lot of yips, so I kept on doing it by myself until they stopped barking. I guess I did okay because I got lots of in-and-out cookies. Yum! My favorite! I can do this forever if they give me cookies! Then I got to play in the yard with my new ball and string toy.

Mama and Daddy didn't have to push me in the doggie door again. I could do it by myself. Not afraid anymore.

He liked his yard, but managed to find something nasty right away.

My yard was fun. Lots of good smells. I found a piece of my stupid sister's leftovers. I wanted to eat it, but Daddy stopped me quick. He said it was "trails." Is it like tails? I didn't have one. Is that the one I lost? Daddy picked it up in a yard spoon. I think he saved it for dinner later. I never saw it again. My stupid sister didn't eat good food like me. I got more than tails. No wonder she's stinky.

 TIPS:

Ease your puppy into new experiences. Make them happy events rather than fearful or stressful ones by giving him lots of treats and praise. Don't force him to do things that may be scary or foreign to him.

Don't overdo the training or the treats. Two to five minutes, depending on the skill, is more than enough time. Constant repetition over the next few weeks will reinforce the behavior.

The Big Green Blanket

We needed to create a nice place for our pup to sleep. We still had the cardboard box, but I wanted him to feel secure with us and not cry through the night. Years earlier, I made a large faux-fur blanket for another dog. The fabric was durable so I took a chance that our pup wouldn't tear it to pieces. This was the best I could manage at the moment.

> I cried for two nights in my box. Mama gave me a "blankie" to keep me company. Baby talk! What's a puppy to do? My big green blanket was special. She said another puppy had it before me. Her name was Blossom. She was a terrier. Mama said she looked a lot like me only smaller. It didn't smell like my stolen sister. Blossom liked the yard. Her blanket smelled like flowers.
>
> She must've been a runt too, if she was smaller. I have to be careful not to be a terror so nobody steals my blanket.
>
> Mama said, "Take good care of the blankie. It's special. Blossom had it for twelve years." I guess I'm safe for that long if I take care of my blanket. Mama called it my Girlfriend. It's warm and soft like my mom, but not the same. I think my mom is lost for good so my blanket will have to do. Not a girl, though. Mama doesn't know a lot. I have to watch her. I made sure I didn't pee on it because it's special. I hope Blossom won't come back for her blanket. I liked it now. A lot.
>
> Just like Blossom, I had my blanket for twelve years. Then we got my sister. But that's another story.

 TIP:

Give your puppy something that will help him adapt to his new home. A bed or blanket will help him feel he has something special of his own.

My New Name

Our pup needed a name. "Bernard, what do you think we should name him?"

He said, "It's up to you. He's *your* puppy!"

I wanted him to have a special name; one that was original. I tested a few out on him. He responded to Duffy best so he helped to choose his own name.

Mama said I'm getting a name. I hoped I could keep this one. My mom used to call me "Uff-uff" at first. She called all of us that, but later she called me "Grrrr!" That was just before she would bite me. Sometimes she dangled me in her face all the way back to our box. I couldn't get out then. I would try, but mom would bark "uff" until I stopped.

My mom's family called us "puppies" but they called me "Oh, no! There he goes again!" I liked that name. They would chase me too. We ran around a lot at mom's house. A lot! Playtime ended when they said they were going to kill me. Then I went back to my box with mom.

Mama said I was special. She said I needed a special name. She called me a lot of names, but I didn't know which one I would get. She said I was an Aussie, but didn't know any Aussie names. I didn't know any Aussies either. What's an Aussie? I thought I was bossy. So confused. She said, "How about an Irish name?" I'm okay with Irish. Irish sounded like a nice name, but she changed her mind. She called me Duffy instead. Now, I have the same name I started with. I don't get it! Maybe my mom told her my name when I wasn't looking.

Yes, I chose my own name, but any name would've been great. Just so I knew they were talking to me. My mom's humans called me "Hey!" a lot. That would've worked too.

First Bath

Duffy's first bath was an ordeal. Bernard and I disagreed on the water temperature. He felt dogs could handle cold water. I thought Duffy should have a warm bath, especially in December, but we tried a cold one in the kitchen sink. After all the flailing and howling, both ours and Duffy's, we decided to try my way the next time!

When I got my first bath, Mama brought a big blanket out. She called it Towel. She put me in a big bowl called Sink and turned on the water. Mama wanted warm, but Daddy said cold. Daddy was alpha dude that day and I got cold water. I was tortured! I thought they were going to stuff me like the turkey we ate. They said it was Thanksgiving. The turkey gave, but nobody said thanks. I saw where they stuffed it too. Uh-uh. No thanks from me either!

I fought hard and cried. "I'm cold! Cold! Let me out!"

I got everybody wet. Everybody barked and growled! Mama put strawberry shampoo on me and rubbed it all over. I got warmer when she rubbed me, but I was still too cold. At least she washed it off. It's embarrassing to smell like food. Like I don't know how to eat.

That was a big day! I wasn't weak, but I didn't like cold water. I showed them how much as best as I could. Everybody tried to get their own way. Nobody listened to me! Mama said that warm water was better. I made sure she got my vote on that! You just have to let your parents know what you want. Humans don't always listen when we have important things to say.

Duffy loved being rubbed dry with his towel. He managed to stand still for a *few* minutes before dashing off to explore something new.

My favorite was Towel. Mama took it outside and rubbed me for a long time. Long. I rolled in it to smell like myself again. My ears felt funny inside. I shook my head. Itchy. Wet. Mama rubbed there too. Daddy said, "You smell like a wet rag." No, that was Towel. I just smelled like food. Mama liked my new smell. She sniffed me a lot. She gave me kisses too. Not like my mom's licks, but good anyway. I still thought I smelled better before. I had to work hard to smell like myself again. I rolled a lot. For a long time. Long!

I played with Towel after my bath. Daddy held it up and I jumped and tugged on it. I ran around until I was dry. Sometimes I pulled Towel around the yard. Mama and Daddy would chase me. Then Mama scratched me with a brush until she got a hairball. She's saving it to make another puppy. She brushed my hair backwards on my tail. Mama called it my rootie-toot because it's short. I was little when somebody pulled my tail off. I didn't see. It hurt, but my mom licked it and made it feel better. Won't grow anymore. Afraid somebody might pull it off again. My tail is smart too.

We even got to play ball until I was dry. We played a long time. Long. Until Mama and Daddy got tired. I liked when we played. Nobody's barking. Just yipping. Everybody's happy. That's a good day! We had a lot of those.

Mama had rules about Towel. When I was small, she'd roll me up in it before taking me outside to dry. I tried running off before she had a chance to dry me, and I got a big long growl for not listening. She pointed to the towel and held me there until I dried up. I didn't know everything she growled, but even my young brain knew she was mad. Don't want to cross Mama. The growling and pointing was easy enough to understand. I got brushed after every bath. I never knew why, and sometimes she pulled hard and my fur hurt, but I could take it. Especially when I got a lot of cookies. I'm a sucker for cookies!

One bath day was particularly memorable. It was the only multiple bath day he had. One I didn't ever want to repeat. By then, Duffy had graduated to the shower. It was back-breaking work so I became particularly infuriated at the outcome.

When I got bigger, Mama gave me baths in the shower. I didn't listen when she said to wait. It was raining outside. Fun! I'm good at the doggie door now. Daddy was watching TV when I ran out. Can't catch me. Mama growled! Loud! Real loud! Never heard her bark that loud!

I had a good time running around and rolling in the mud. Didn't need Towel. Too much fun! Mama was mad! Real mad!

Daddy said, "It's okay. Use the towel."

Mama's too mad to listen. She grabbed me hard! Just like my mom. Mama dangled me by my neck. I sat in her paws. I didn't move. Scary! She was so mad she would've killed me for sure! I wanted to cry, but had to be brave.

That day I had two baths. I got smelly stuff two times! Mama said "Wait!" a lot. It means listen or else. Else means Death. I got lucky and only got another bath. No kisses today. Just lots of loud barking in my sore ears. Don't know all she said, but she kept growling "Wait!" No cookies either. No playing outside with Towel. Even Daddy stayed far. Mama rules on bath day.

Sometimes fun to me wasn't fun to my parents. I got that down real quick. About the only mud I got on myself after that was on my paws. Even then I had to wait to get washed off. Mama and Daddy are good about a lot of things, but mud isn't one of them.

🐾 TIPS:

Dogs like warm baths. Bathe them regularly, though brushing your dog may mean bathing him less. Brushing reduces dirt and stimulates the oils in his coat that bathing would otherwise remove.

Ease your puppy into the bath experience. Use a shallow tub the first time. Be prepared to ease his stress with treats and lots of praise.

Dry him with a large towel. Teach him to use the towel instead of running off into the grass or mud to roll.

Start grooming your puppy at an early age so he'll learn to enjoy, or at least tolerate, it.

Siblings

Our cat and Duffy got along well. Duffy seemed to accept her as a surrogate mother. Jingles tolerated Duffy well enough to nap with him nearby. He was still hyperactive and rambunctious, but surprisingly conciliatory to her, even at meal time.

Jingles never had it so good. She used to lie around on the house grass. I taught her to get on the nice sofa and Daddy's chair, but you better be off when he's around or there's "hell to pay." We sat and slept on the sofa most days. Pillows were nice. Mama hid them under a blanket, but I knew where they lived. I could lie upside down with my paws on them. Soft.

At night, I slept on the bed because I'm good. My stupid sister slept there only when Mama and Daddy went out. We'd sneak in. Sneak. They didn't want a stinky bed. They threw her out at night. I rolled on her spot so they didn't know she was there. They couldn't smell her, so we're safe. Our secret.

Jingles liked to eat my food. Daddy said, "Jingles is a goner" the first time, but I let her eat some. If she took too long, I'd say "uff-uff" and bang her on the back with my paw so she'd get out of the way.

Mama said, "See, he's not uncouth. Duffy's got manners."

Hmmm. That day, I learned "couth." I didn't mind unless Jingles had rat breath.

Jingles ate lots of fresh food. She must've gone to "Petco where the pets go." Daddy said it was a lizard this time. Didn't smell like chicken. She wasn't going to share. It's okay.

Mama didn't like what she saw. "Eww!" she said. "That's disgusting!"

Jingles ate everything but the stuffing. Daddy picked that up with his yard spoon. He put it in a can to give to the neighbors. I didn't mind rolling on it, but I wouldn't eat it. Uh-uh. No way. Mama neither. No couth!

🐾 TIPS:

Be aware of your dog's fondness for rolling on nasty things. Most of these items smell bad and are full of bacteria. You don't want these germs or smells in your home.

Keep the hair between his pads short and check your dog's paws after he's been outside to minimize dirt and debris from being tracked into the house.

Cat Food

Once Duffy was allowed to roam the entire house, it was time to move Jingles' food bowl. Bernard decided to feed Jingles in our spare room. It worked well enough unless Duffy managed to sneak in for a bite. Duffy discovered he loved her food so much that he inhaled the entire bowl before she could eat. His explorations sometimes led to other discoveries.

Daddy moved Jingles' secret stash to a room where only they could go. She never brought me any. I waited at the secret door for her, but she just ran away when I did. I almost caught her once when she ran into the wall, but no food came out. Sad.

I walked up close one day and got a bite before Daddy chased me out. Yum! Gourmet food! Mama said it's fish! Yum! Fish! My new favorite! I was going to share with Mama, but I forgot and ate it myself. Cat food is my favorite!

There's more good stuff in a big rock box too. Daddy said it's a litter box. It's not so little. It's big! Mama said it's "No,

Duffy. Bad!" I tried, though. Sneak, sneak. Not enough time to find anything good.

Over the years, Daddy and I ran to see who could get to Jingles' stash first. He'd fill her bowl and I'd check out the box. Then he'd push me away and I'd jump on the food bowl. I didn't get in all the time, but whenever I did, I'd eat what I could get.

Daddy made me laugh. He would growl and swat at me. He missed most of the time. That was the best game!

Jingles knew not to stand in the doorway when I got in. I flipped her when I went in and trampled her when I came out. I think Jingles liked eating out better. She didn't get beat up so much. Yeah, those were great times!

🐾 TIPS:

Most dogs love cat food. You can indulge them with a few pieces of cat kibble once in a while, but cat food has much more fat than dog food.

Your dog should eat food that's formulated for him. If you have a puppy, feed him puppy food. Adult and senior pets have other dietary requirements. Be an avid label reader to make sure he's getting what he needs. Check with your vet if you have any questions about diet.

Dogs like to go litter box diving. Keep them out of the boxes. They love the "cat treats," but the bacteria and possible toxins from the litter itself could be harmful to your dog. Litter that clumps can cause a blockage that may require surgery.

Quiet Evenings at Home

Duffy was never still and played with unending zeal. When he started losing his milk teeth, we became his chew toys. After many bloody scratches and punctures to our hands, arms, legs, and Bernard's nose, we decided we needed armor. Bernard purchased a pair of tough leather gloves for those wild evening romps. Even after exhausting us, Duffy managed to find new and inventive ways to amuse himself.

Daddy and I played a game every night. He tried to whack me and I'd grab his paw covers if he missed. Mama called them Gloves. Daddy missed a lot, so I chewed his gloves to make my mouth feel better.

Mama said, "Duffy's losing his baby teeth." She called me baby a lot. It's okay if I got cookies. Yum! My favorite!

The gloves were for the fireplace, but we didn't have one so I was the next best thing. The gloves were soft. Daddy said "ouch" a lot when I bit them. He barked and growled real loud. Stuff Mama said shouldn't be barked in public. One time I got to swing from the gloves for a long time. Long. Daddy couldn't get me off. I had fun until my tooth let go. I lost a couple more puppy teeth in them, but it didn't hurt. Mama kept them. She said they're mementos. Mama's confused a lot. They're really teeth, even though I heard her say Toes. They're Toes if I get cookies! Yum!

One night Daddy was sitting in his "hell to pay" chair with his paws up. I wanted to play. I jumped over his paws and landed on his face. His mouth was open wide like he was going to eat me. Too late. I licked him, but my face went in his mouth and my tongue went up to his brains. Mama laughed real hard. For a long time. Long. She said I launched at Daddy. Lunch? I kept looking for lunch, but didn't get any. My puppy brain knew Lunch. So I thought Mama was confused again.

Daddy was gagging and choking and had to drink water. Lots of water. Lots. He said he could still taste me!

He said, "Yuck! I know where that tongue's been."

Yep. Me too. We all saw it. That was fun and Mama was happy. Real happy. I could tell. Me too! That was fun! I'll have to do it again.

There were a lot of nights my parents would play with me and my toys. I would bump things like the coffee table. I don't know why they called it that because we never ate coffee on it. What's coffee? It's a No-Coffee Table. Just food. And cookies! Yum! Daddy wrapped bandages on its paws so it wouldn't cry when I bumped it. Coffee Table isn't tough like me. Mama's slow and not so tough, either. She bumped it a few times and said "ow." She can't see too good. I had to help her. A lot.

Later, Mama and Daddy got me bones. They called them rawhide, but I knew a bone when I saw one. I got to chew one every night. Daddy said, "Better the rawhide than me!" He was happy because I didn't bite his gloves anymore. "They're ripped to shreds!" I thought they were perfect. Nice holes for my pretty new teeth.

Those were good times when I was a carefree puppy. As I got older, we still had fun, but most days I chewed on my bone while my parents sat around. They didn't like to play much anymore. They're not Aussies. Old too. Old. At least ten.

🐾 TIPS:

You will be the object of your puppy's chewing affection because of his natural desire to be near you. Be especially careful to keep him away from your face.

Children, because they're low to the ground, are easy targets for sharp puppy teeth.

Keep inappropriate chewing down by trading a toy for his chosen object for destruction. His need to chew is greatest when he's ready to lose his milk teeth.

Chapter 3

Necessary Evils

The Vet

I made an appointment to take Duffy for a complete checkup a week after I brought him home. The veterinarian we visited so many years ago was located many miles away, so I chose a clinic in our neighborhood for the convenience without learning of their reputation beforehand. Since Duffy had a tendency to panic when we rode in the car, the closer clinic was important to ease the stress on all of us. Bernard elected not to go since it should've been an easy visit. So I thought.

The veterinary technician who greeted us was friendly and gentle with Duffy. He managed to calm Duffy's initial fears and recorded a few preliminary notes before the veterinarian appeared.

Duffy started to struggle when he met the veterinarian. The harder he fought, the harder the vet held him. I saw his fingers digging into Duffy's little body until he screamed. The vet deliberately hurt my puppy! I was so disturbed by the whole experience that I vowed never to go back!

Mama and the Car took me to a scary place. I didn't like the Car. The Car was not my friend! I knew for sure now the Car was Trouble! It took me to the Vet. The place smelled bad. Everybody was scared when they came here. I knew the smell. I was afraid and shaking so much my tongue leaked. The Vet came to see me and put me on a cold table. I wanted to jump off, but it was too high and I was weak from shaking. He caught me and held me as I fought hard to get down. Mama let me cry. She didn't care. He wasn't holding her. He put me in a bowl real quick, and I thought this is the end. Good-bye. But he said, "Let's get his weight."

Confused. How do you "get" when you have to "wait"? My young brain didn't understand.

He said, "12 pounds."

I guess I get 12 pounds. Not fat enough to eat so we have to wait.

Another Vet came and hurt me. I didn't like him. He's bad! He held me hard until I screamed.

When we left, Mama promised not to go back and told Daddy the Vet was too rough.

I said "ruff," too, and Daddy laughed.

Mama said the Vet manhandled me. He squeezed hard. I thought I was going to pop. Who's Man Hand? I don't get it. They called him the Vet. I don't want to see the Vet again. I was just a puppy. Traumatized. I smelled fear everywhere! Why wouldn't I be scared? I'm glad we didn't go back. Mama felt bad so I got cookies. Lots. Yum!

🐾 TIPS:

Choose your vet carefully. Get recommendations. Don't just pick one because the location is convenient. Your pup's first experience with the vet sets the tone for future visits.

Make your first visit to the vet short and fun. Take your puppy for a visit to the vet before undergoing a full exam with shots. Some vets will give you a tour so your pup will have a positive first experience.

Bumble Bees

I heard a funny sound in the yard one day and saw a big black ball fly by. I chased it. All over the yard.

Daddy barked and said "Leave it," but it was a ball! I ran to bite it. The ball was slow so I caught it. The ball made my face shake.

Daddy said I had a bumble bee. He called it B-52. He counts a lot of bees. I liked it in my mouth. I let it go because it made my tongue tickle. The Bumble Ball was all wet and couldn't fly too good after that. Up and down all over.

Daddy said, "You're lucky you didn't get stung!" What's stung?

I found out soon enough. I played with the Bumble Bee without getting stung the first time, but wasn't so lucky after that. Since then, everything that poked or stung reminded me of that Bumble Bee!

The New Vet

We discovered another veterinarian close by, in the opposite direction from the last one. I didn't want any reminders of that other horrible vet!

Duffy was in no mood to ride in the car again, but his next encounter with a bumble bee gave us no choice. Bernard drove as Duffy flung himself all over the back seat and screamed in desperation. I held his leash, but couldn't control him. When our car came to a halt at an intersection, the drama in the car escalated. His protestations became ear-piercing yikes as he tried to claw his way out of the two-inch window opening in the car. Passengers in adjacent vehicles gave us disapproving glances as the chaos intensified.

"What are those people doing to that poor puppy?" they wondered. Embarrassed and frustrated, our three-way shrill chorus did nothing to placate those disapproving observers from thinking badly of us.

I saw the Bumble Bee again. The Bumble Bee poked me inside my face. My face got fat. Mama took me to the Vet to get shot. I was afraid, but couldn't fight too hard. My face hurt and my nose got fat too. Hard to breathe. I couldn't see so good because my nose got in the way. If the Vet popped me now, I won't see it happen.

The Vet was a lady this time. She was nice. She didn't hurt me, but I was too scared to notice. I couldn't see because my face was shaking and my tongue was leaking. All over the place. I was still screaming, but not as loud now.

Daddy picked me up and carried me on the scale. Wow! 250 pounds! Mama wrote down twenty-eight. I was 12 pounds with the last Vet, but Mama fed me lots of cookies when he hurt me. I'm okay now.

The Vet looked inside my face and said she was going to shoot me. I was afraid. I guess they're going to kill me after all. Mama couldn't save me with twenty-eight. Rooo! Good-bye! I was so scared I wanted to pee, but only my tongue would pee.

Everybody felt bad for me. I guess this is good-bye. The Vet felt bad too. The Vet touched my face and nose before she poked me on my back. She found my Bumble Bee and made it poke me again. Not fair!

Mama and Daddy took me home to sleep. I wanted cookies, but they just let me lie on my sofa to starve.

Later, Daddy made barbecue and Mama gave me some steak because she felt bad. I could see better and my face wasn't fat anymore. I was just weak from being starved.

I looked for my Bumble Bee every day, but he didn't come anymore. He stayed with the Vet.

As I look back, it was pretty funny that I thought I weighed 250 pounds. Daddy got on the scale with me, so I really was twenty-eight. I thought Mama was trying to save me from death. It took me a long time to figure out a shot was that nasty bee I kept getting every time I went to the Vet. You never see it coming!

One good thing about getting a fat face is how guilty you can make your parents feel. I gave them my saddest look, and they kept feeding me steak. Told you I was smart.

Duffy didn't understand the vet visits were for his own good. Shortly after the bee sting incident, we reluctantly returned for Duffy's booster shots. It meant freedom from the confines of our backyard, but it also meant another upsetting car ride for the three of us. The drama unfolded predictably, and we were completely frazzled by the time we dragged him through the door. He was barely four months old! How will we manage when he's full-grown?

Mama and Daddy took me to the Vet again for my boo shots. Scary! Rooo! I'm in Trouble again. I was stuck in the back with the Car Pet, but I was the only one screaming. The humans in the car next to us knew Mama and Daddy were going to kill me. I cried for help, but they just looked at me and my parents. Mama said I was embarrassing.

Daddy started barking at me to "Shut up!" Mama kept saying, "Stop!" We barked all the way to the Vet.

The Vet came in with a Bumble Bee like the one in our yard and gave me a couple of boo shots. Mama called them boosters. One went up my nose and I had to lick my face because it ran back out. Tasted bad, but it had no place to go, so my tongue was as good as any. The Vet gave me a cookie, and I felt a little better. They weren't good cookies like ours. She must not know "Petco where the pets go." My tongue stopped leaking, though.

It was time to go and I was ready to run away, but I couldn't get too far with only two paws on the ground. Daddy took me to the car where I whined to the Car Pet. I was hoping it would feel bad for me. No luck. He must be afraid of Trouble too.

Trouble brought us home. Safe again! I was happy to see my new squeaky toy and sofa. They waited for me to come home.

🐾 **TIPS:**

When your dog is barking loudly, don't add to the clamor. Speak softly and calmly. He'll be more likely to quiet down to hear you.

The Big Snip

This was not a moment I relished. Our vet said Duffy should be neutered to help him be a better family dog. He'd be less likely to wander or mark his territory. A few health issues could be averted, and he might even become a calmer dog. *Calm!* That word alone convinced me this procedure should be done.

My emotions got the best of me that fateful morning. Duffy and I both cried our way to the vet. At six months of age, Duffy was still a puppy.

Bernard assured me, "He'll be fine. It's a simple operation. They'll take good care of him." Bernard was a rock in tough circumstances. He always knew the right thing to do or say.

The surgery went well, but Duffy was a groggy little puppy when we returned for him. The vet placed a large cone around his head to prevent him from ripping his stitches. Duffy's head drooped from the weight of the cone as he wobbled all the way to the car. This contraption stayed with him for nearly two weeks until we returned to have his stitches removed. In the meantime, Duffy recovered in two days and played without doing damage to himself or the house.

Mama and Daddy had a secret. They didn't tell me. I think they're going to eat me now. I heard Mama say I'm old enough. Rooo! I liked it here. Not fair. I'm a good boy.

They stuffed me in Trouble and I cried. Mama too. I knew this was good-bye. My parents didn't love me after all. I missed my ball. And string toy. Oh, no! We're going to the Vet! The Vet's going to kill me with the Bumble Bee. I knew it. That's why everybody's afraid there. Why didn't they eat my stupid sister instead of me? I'm smart. She's stupid. She wouldn't know the difference.

The Vet pulled me inside the spooky place. I fought hard, but my butt brakes didn't work. My rootie-toot was too short. I was doomed. Doomed. Two Vets put me on a table. I knew they were going to shoot me with the Bumble Bee. I was shaking, and my tongue was leaking. All over the table. They tried to be nice, but I knew better. They ate my paw hair with a kazillion Bumble Bees. I guess that's for their dinner later. Good-bye, ball. Good-bye, string toy. No good-bye to Mama and Daddy, though. They're mean! My head and eyes fell down. Sleepy. Good. I didn't want to look anyway.

I woke up again. I still smelled the Vet. There's lots of noise. They haven't killed me yet. More puppies were here. Maybe they're next. If they eat them first, they might be too full to eat me. I felt funny, and my paw hurt. Eeek! The Bumble Bee is still there. A string toy is on it, but not like my string toy. Too sleepy. My butt hurt. I looked. Couldn't see. It hurt to lift my paw. I wanted to cry, but had to be brave. I hurt. Too sleepy to fight. I had to pee, but couldn't get up. Weak. I needed a cookie. I was hungry and nobody cared. Sleepy.

The Vet laid me on the table. I was too weak to fight. She pulled the Bumble Bee out. String toy was gone now. She made me walk. My back paws hugged my butt. Whine! Couldn't walk too good. It hurt. Still sleepy.

Mama and Daddy came back. My rootie-toot wanted to say hi, but that hurt too. The Vet put a big can on my neck. She called it e-collar. I didn't like it. I shook and hit it with my paw, but it wouldn't come off. The Vet told Mama to keep it on for a couple of weeks. How come I have to wear it when the Vet said Mama had to keep it? The Vet said I had stitches. Hmmm. Stitches. I know Stitches! Mama stitches my toys when the stuffing comes out. I guess my stuffing was coming out. Mama didn't want Daddy to get his yard spoon. I'd be dinner. So sad. Nobody had this can but me. Embarrassing. I didn't look at anybody when we left.

We came home to my ball and string toy. Jingles wasn't around. For once, she's smart. Mama and Daddy said they felt bad I got fixed. What did they fix? My stuffing wasn't hanging out before. Maybe they saw something I missed. They stuffed me too tight. No running. It hurt. For a long time. Two days.

We went back to the Vet. I hoped the Vet would take her can back. I couldn't see anything with it on. I banged things a lot. I couldn't fit in the dog door. Couldn't check my stuffing. My rootie-toot felt better though. It could say "hi" again.

Eek! Eek! The Vets held me upside down. I fought hard, but they fought harder. They pulled the string toy out. I checked if my stuffing came out. That happened a lot to my toys. Then Daddy puts them in a can and I never see them again. All gone. My stuffing had to stay in good. I didn't want it to be gone. At least they took my big can. I still don't know what they fixed. I'm still the same. Cute. Smart. Genius.

Annual Checkups

Every year, we tried to be inventive getting Duffy in and out of the vet's office with our sanity intact. We were never successful.

We went to the Vet real early one day, Daddy said, "So we get in first." Nobody was around. I got to read the doggie mail in their yard. Boring. Every mail was worried. Me too! We still waited.

Soon, the Vet said, "Come on in."

Daddy opened the door and a lady with two fat puppies ran in first. Mama was mad at Daddy for being polite. I didn't see Polite. Who's Polite? I only saw the lady with the fat puppies. We had to wait again. I wanted to go home so I barked and pulled a lot until Daddy said "obnoxious" and went outside. Just Mama and me now. She kissed me to make me feel better. Not working.

The lady's puppies had eggs for heads. Maybe they ate my Bumble Bee. Mama said they were bull terriers. I said "rooo," but they ran to the Vet without a sniff. Stupid dogs. They ran the wrong way! I sniffed where they walked, but it wasn't the same.

Toothache

Duffy was five when we found a big lump on his face. He hadn't been stung by a bee again so we knew something odd had happened. We made an appointment with the vet and prepared ourselves for another earsplitting ride in the car.

The vet examined him and discovered he had an abscess in a cracked tooth. All the years of chewing on tree bark and rawhide took its toll. The vet decided it would be best to remove the tooth. The extraction didn't take long, but when we returned, Duffy cried and made us feel very guilty for leaving him.

I got Ab's Sis in my tooth. I didn't know Ab, but his sis was bad. I had a Bumble Bee face again, but different. It hurt inside my face where my food goes. My parents gave me to the Vet. I guess this time I'm a goner. Not perfect anymore. Good-bye. Afraid. I stood my ground, but I couldn't get my butt brakes to work. I slipped all over the floor and left skid marks on the way. Choking and crying. Nobody cared. My parents left without me. Waah! Rooo!

The Vet poked me with the Bumble Bee again. I stayed a long time. Long. All day.

When my parents finally came for me, I was too scared and weak to yip. My rootie-toot didn't say "hi." I missed my bed. The Vet's house scares me. My face still hurt. I saw my tongue leaking, but I didn't feel it. Ab's Sis must've taken it.

🐾 TIPS:

Throughout your dog's life, there will be minor emergencies and necessary procedures that call for visits to the vet. Be firm but loving to your pet. Don't add to his fears by reinforcing his behavior. Be calm. He'll feed off your body language and emotional energy.

Spaying and neutering, though seemingly barbaric to some, helps prevent potential health problems later in your dog's life. If your puppy will be a family pet, this procedure should be considered as a means of limiting unwanted puppies and dogs that overburden shelters every day.

Chapter 4

Learning the Rules

Leash Training

We purchased the tiniest pale blue collar and leash for Duffy at the pet store soon after I brought him home. The clerk showed us a reflector tag I thought would be a good idea to have. Duffy was hard to see in the yard at night with his mostly-black coat.

He resisted the collar and tag at first, but he soon forgot he had it on. He looked quite debonair. I couldn't wait to show him off to the world. First, he had to learn to walk on-leash. I felt sorry for the little guy because he always wanted to go and we kept pulling him back to stay with us. It seemed like punishment for a spirited dog. We tried to make him understand the leash was for his own good, even as we watched him thrash and flop around to get out of its control. Duffy eventually learned to tolerate the leash on his walks, but he never stopped pulling. Eventually we ended up using a choke chain.

My parents tortured me a lot the next few weeks. They got a neck rope called Collar for me. And a tag that Mama said glows in the dark so she can see me. I can see me fine, but she doesn't see too good. Like the can, it's for her, but I have to wear it. It was nice at first, but they put a string they called Leash on it and yanked me all around the yard. I liked to run ahead, but they wanted me to stay close. I saw a lot of things two or three times. Sometimes I'd fly by them, and then fly back. That's fun if I'm not choking.

Sometimes I got to read doggie mail, but I had to be fast. Mama said I take too long to sniff so we live by the five-second rule. Daddy taught me that. If any goodies dropped on the floor, Daddy would say, "Five-second rule!" That meant it's still good. Then we'd both jump to get it. I liked that rule! Mama would just shake her head.

I found yard treats too, but I had to eat fast. She'd get mad and say, "I have to fish that out!" Then Mama made me gag.

She'd say, "Eww!" and wipe her hand after fishing. A lot. Mama said it's disgusting so I fly by, but I don't get to fly back.

I liked my doggie mail. Mama and Daddy only read the mail that came in a box by the door. Mr. Reynolds brought it. Not much good in that mail. Must be stuff he didn't want. Mama called them bills. My parents didn't look happy so I guess the news was bad. I only found good mail. Lots. That's why I'm smart. I read a lot.

After I learned my flybys and flybacks, we went past the wall they called Gate. Only I had to wear my collar and leash. Mama said I always have to be dressed when we go out. I don't like my dress.

Being choked by a leash was bad. Bad! They wanted me to be like my brothers and sisters. Boring. I think that's what my mom tried to tell me. Independence was hard to come by.

Humans have a lot of rules. Do this; don't do that. You can eat this, but for heaven's sake don't eat that! Walk with me. Don't sniff so long! Humans need to stop and smell the roses. Or at least check out the neighborhood mail.

🐾 TIPS:

Choose the right equipment for leash training. A dog's throat is very delicate. Hard tugging can injure your dog. Start with a Gentle Leader or harness to save wear and tear on you and your dog.

Entice him with treats or a toy to help him accept his new collar and leash.

Don't allow your dog to forcefully pull on his walks. If he does pull, go the other way. You may be walking back and forth in a short space for a while, but this will teach him who's walking whom. *You* need to control the journey.

Playing tug-of-war on walks with your dog doesn't work. You'll always lose. Call your dog to you and change directions. The more you pull, the harder he'll pull. Soon, you won't be able to handle him because he's now in control.

Grooming

We received a lot of advice on our first visit to the pet store. Besides the Wee-Wee Pads and Nature's Miracle, the salesclerk suggested we get a brush and shampoo. Over time, I discovered grooming shears, nail clippers, and even a toothbrush and toothpaste.

The shampoo and brush came in handy from the very beginning and Duffy enjoyed the attention that came after his bath. Clipping his nails became a test of wills and a huge learning curve on my part. As a pup, Duffy disliked having his feet handled, and one time he zigged when I zagged and I cut too much nail and made his toe bleed. At the time, I didn't know about styptic pencils or powder to stop the bleeding. He reinjured his toe on his walk that day, and we had to carry him home. I thought I'd injured him for life, even though he forgave me for my carelessness.

As the years passed, I groomed him regularly and became relatively proficient with his trims. He sported a short bob on his rear end during the summer months. Bernard said he liked the trim.

"He looks like a girl," he joked. Duffy wasn't perturbed. He knew he looked great.

The toothbrush and toothpaste weren't introduced until after his extraction. Before then, we faithfully took him in for cleanings, but worried when he was under anesthesia. The new tools gave us more time between cleanings, even though his teeth were brushed only once a week.

When I was a puppy, Mama got a brush at "Petco where the pets go." Every time she pawed me with it, I got itchy. Sometimes it tickled, but mostly I got itchy. My paw would go up and down a lot. Mama would laugh when it did. Me too. I made her happy all the time. She gave me cookies when she was done, and she told me I was pretty. I liked that. Even though boys aren't supposed to be pretty. I liked it almost as much as my towel, but I didn't have to get a bath to get brushed. Good.

Mama discovered something called shears. The first time she decided to cut me with them I was afraid, but she gave me cookies. Mmmm! I love cookies!

Snip! Yike! She stole my butt hair with it. Small noise but scary. I wanted to see. Mama kept pushing me around. Snip! Hey! I want to see. I don't want to miss something important. I don't want something important missing either! I have to use that.

Mama pushed me back. She growled. No cookie. She called Daddy. He said, "I'm not having any of that!" I was thinking the same, but I was trapped. What's Mama having?

Snip! "Owwooo!" I whined. Mama said I'm a big baby! I tried to be brave. She only cut my hair. I said it wasn't me. My hair said it. Snip! Okay, no oww. I sighed. Nothing hurt but my feelings. Mama would see my sad eyes and give me a cookie. Hmmm! I kept looking sad. I got tons of cookies by looking sad. At least five! Mama's cheap, though. She broke them up so it looked like a lot, but I know. I can count. One, snap, snap. Two, snap. Three, snap, snap, snap. Four, snap. Five, snap, snap. See? She gave me the little stuff too, but too small to be cookies. Mama called them Crumbs. Because they fell on the floor. The five-second-rule cookies never count.

Mama's finished. No more cookies. I'd try to check out the bag, but Mama pushed me away again. That's what I thought. Cheap.

"No more cookies. You don't want to get fat," Mama said. How can I get fat when I'm starving to death? Daddy thinks I look cute. Well, yeah! Just wait, Daddy. Mama might cut your butt hair next.

Mama said I had a butt bob. Who's Bob? Lots of air behind. Weird. I look, but nothing's there. Eek! Eek! Nothing's there! Eek! Where's my hair? Somebody stole my hair! Mama has it! She stuffed my hair in a bag for dinner later! Maybe she's saving it to make a puppy. I ran around and rolled. I needed my hair back! Worried. Like my tail, gone for good. Had hair today, but what's gone tomorrow? They're going to eat me in little pieces. Waah! Rooo!

Now Mama has another weapon! She said it's a nail clipper. Wait! I don't have nails. Why is she grabbing my paw? What's a Nail? I didn't take a nail. Wasn't me! I screamed. They planned to kill me for a nail I didn't have! Maybe she said mail. She can sniff or lick my paws and read the mail without cutting them. I do it all the time!

Daddy came to help, but not me. He grabbed me so I couldn't run. It's a trap! Not fair! Yike! Yike! I fought hard, but Daddy held tight. Mama's going to cut off my paw! Yike! I pulled away, but Mama held tight too! Snip! Crunch! Yike! Owwooo! That time it did hurt! She cut my paw! I know it! Snip! Crunch! Yike! Whine, whine! No cookies! Just hurt!

Mama said, "It's okay. Stop whining!"

I worried. Not okay. I can't walk without my paws! Why my paws? I'm a good boy! Nobody gave me cookies. Too busy killing me. I cried a long time. Long. At least five minutes. Mama and Daddy grunted the whole time! They finally let go. I walked. My paw was okay. Other paws okay. Not hurt, but my toes felt funny. The front isn't touching the ground anymore. Weird. How did they do that? I ran to see if my toes could touch the ground. Okay now, but nobody remembered my cookies. I ran to the cookie door, but nobody was watching. I tried to look sad, but no luck either. Everybody's lying down and panting but me.

One day Mama wasn't so nice with the nail clipper. We fought again. The clipper bit me. Hard! My toe is gone for sure. I knew there was blood all over. Even in the neighbor's yard! A kazillion miles away. I yiked and cried. Whine, whine. Mama said, "Oh, baby, I'm so sorry!" Not as sorry as me. I'm bleeding to death and nobody cares.

She gave me a whole cookie this time. Yum! I liked cookies! More, more! I almost forgot my toe hurt.

Mama said she cut too quick. She wiped up the two drops of blood on the ground that I tried to lick. See! I'm bleeding to death. Hey! That's mine! I might need that. I guess that goes in the dinner later. Along with my toe. Mama still called it Nail, but it looked like a toe to me. She squeezed it hard so I wouldn't feel anything, but I knew my toe was gone.

Good-bye.

Another weapon came home after I lost my tooth to Ab's sis. Now what? Mama tortured me a lot. Just so she could say I looked pretty. I had to admit I'm pretty, but didn't let it get around. I had a reputation to protect. She said it's a toothbrush. She put something like peanut butter on it. Only it doesn't taste like peanut butter. It tastes like chicken. Not bad. I don't know why I had to eat it on that stick, though. I can lick it up without it. Mama's not too smart sometimes. Mama shook the stick and it tickled inside my face. It made Mama happy so I just pretended she knew what she's doing. Secret.

 TIPS:

Brushing your dog may mean bathing him less. Use a soft brush and gently stroke him with it. Reward him with treats.

Nail trimming is not something he will tolerate early on. Dogs generally don't like their feet handled so just touching their paws regularly will allow you to ease into trimming. Dremels are gentler on the nails than clippers. Get him used to the sound first before using it on his nails. Have styptic powder on hand in case you trim too close and his nail bleeds.

Your dog needs dental care as well. Dog toothpaste is usually chicken or beef flavored. Put some on a finger brush or toothbrush and let him make first contact. He'll think it's a treat. You need to ease into this as well. It's better to prevent dental problems than pay hefty fees for cleanings and dental work as he ages.

Early detection of anomalies on his skin, paws, ears, and mouth can be made when you groom him regularly.

A Walk in the Park

After he received his booster shots, we dressed Duffy in his finery and ventured out for his first walk. We went to a nearby park, hoping to find other dogs for him to meet. It took us a while to get there since he found so many new smells to explore. Some odors were so interesting he became mesmerized by the scents, and we finally set rules to keep him moving. We learned to avert many germy or rotten little "delicacies" he found along the route. The downside would be digging them out of his mouth before he swallowed it.

Duffy loved the park and his new friends. The people we met were enamored by our cute bundle of energy. He ran and herded everyone, including their dogs. He'd come in for a quick pat or two before running off again. He especially liked Lee, an older woman with overweight dogs. She brought entire boxes of cookies and happily dispensed them to every dog within arm's reach. Naturally, Duffy gravitated to her often.

Wow! We have a lot bigger yard than I thought. This part is called the Park. I was a happy boy! We went far! At least two blocks! Far! I met a lot of new puppies and their humans. They all tried to catch me, but I'm fast. Everybody loved me because I'm cute. Mama said, "You're the darling of the park!" I loved everybody because they gave me cookies and hugs. Yum! Hugs were okay, but I liked cookies better. My favorite! I could eat cookies all day.

One human named Lee gave me lots of cookies. Mama said, "Too much!" She doesn't want me to get fat like Lee's dogs. Lee said they're terriers, but Mama said they're sausages. Somebody could eat them soon. I guess I'm not a sausage so they didn't eat me. I think Mama liked me around. She held me tight a lot.

Daddy liked me around too. He yipped and barked at me all the time, even though he liked my stupid sister better, but he said, "Sometimes I think nobody's home behind those eyes." I don't get it. She's home. Is Nobody with her?

She doesn't go with us to the Park. They didn't bring her because she's stinky. Embarrassing!

Friends at the Park

During his juvenile period, we realized he didn't play like the other dogs who would take turns chasing or being chased by each other. Duffy couldn't control his speed. Most little dogs couldn't keep up so he ran into them. Once they rolled, he would step on them. His "king of the hill" attitude was not acceptable.

Several dog owners exited the park in a huff because of his behavior with their dogs. He ran alongside larger dogs, but barked in their ears as he steered them around the park. He even intimidated these dogs.

Then he met a speedy Greyhound named McKenzie. Duffy finally met his match! He chased her several times around the park until he crumpled in an exhausted heap. We hoped she'd come more often. Disgruntled dog owners mentioned her when Duffy was a puppy. As much as we hoped she'd come back often, he only played with her twice.

Only one dog managed to put him in his place. She was a medium-sized female about five years old named Ginger. Duffy's boisterous ways got him a healthy nip. He learned a good lesson and she was the only dog he minded for a long time.

That name cropped up again in his life. I wondered if that name was as significant to him as it was to us.

Soon, Duffy's circle of friends diminished to Lee's dogs, Rusty and Dusty, who ignored Duffy's urges to play, and Ricky the beagle, who enjoyed the romps with Duffy, though we didn't see them every day.

We hadn't seen Ricky for several weeks. By then, we learned he had been attacked by a pit bull running loose in the park one day. His injuries were very serious and, even after he healed, he couldn't run in the park anymore. As Duffy's reputation spread, dog owners would leave the park when we arrived, so he eventually spent his playtime in solitude.

I made a lot of new friends. Rusty, Dusty, Sassy, Scarlett, McKenzie, Ricky, and Ginger. Ginger was like my mom. I jumped on Ginger and she bit me. Not as hard as mom, but she barked my other name, "Grrrr!" How did she know? I stayed far after that. I had to watch her. She's grumpy if you jumped on her. Sometimes she looked at me and I stayed far. Safer. Grumpy. Must get grumpy when you get old. Her mama said Ginger was five.

Ricky was the only one who played with me a lot. Most of my new friends didn't like to play. I'm fast. Nobody could keep up. I liked to chase them and bark in their ear. All around the park. If they stopped, I ran them over. Fun! The small puppies rolled and rolled.

Then everybody barked at me. I don't get it. Maybe because I held them down. Still, I'm a cute puppy so they loved me anyway.

Rusty and Dusty were sausage terriers. They barked a lot and didn't run very far. We played, but they liked to stay with the treats. Their mama, Lee, brought a kazillion boxes of treats for us. At least one. We didn't go too far when she had her box.

McKenzie was the most fun. Mama said she's a Greyhound, but she's brown. McKenzie ran really fast. Nobody liked her. Maybe because she's bigger than me and ran over their puppies too. Everybody but me ran away when McKenzie came to the park.

I'm getting bigger. My friends stayed small and their humans got mad if I ran over their puppies. Daddy said my body slam hurt their dogs. Wimpy! Not tough like me. I heard, "Here comes Duffy," and they'd leave the park. Just like with McKenzie before. I'm sad. No friends and no cookies anymore unless Lee's there, but Mama and Daddy would bring a ball for me to chase so I'm okay. The ball is faster anyway. I ran far. And I got to jump high.

Sometimes the dog catcher came and everybody ran, even us. I don't know why. He liked to play too, but he's too slow. He couldn't catch me. Might catch Mama, though. Don't want him to take her. So we all disappeared. Lee said she got fined once and Mama and Daddy felt bad. I don't get it. Lee's happy when I find her. That's because I smelled her cookies. Yum! My favorite!

I liked playing with Ricky, but one day his boy said he got hurt in the park. A pit bull bit him and he had surgery. The next time I saw him, he couldn't run and play. He was all tied up like my Coffee Table so he walked funny. He was my best friend, but he didn't come to the park anymore. Sad, but I still have my ball.

I spent a lot of time playing ball with my parents at the park. Nobody wanted to play with my ball. One day I jumped real high and hurt my paw. Daddy carried me home. It hurt, but I didn't cry. It was a long trip because I didn't lead the way. Mama felt real bad. I could tell. Her heart was sad. Daddy too.

Mama whined at the phone. Then they stuffed me in Trouble. I knew my life was over. Not a perfect puppy anymore. I could smell the Vet all the way from the stoplight! I cried a lot then, but nobody cared. Except the humans in the next car. Maybe they'll save me! "Help! Help! Rooo!" I pawed at the window so they would see me. They only looked at Mama and Daddy.

We got to the Vet's house. I tried my butt brakes. My paw hurt so Daddy won this time. My tongue was leaking again, and my face was shaking. The Vet grabbed my paw. I didn't like that. She pulled and didn't let go. Yike! She was going to eat me paw first. She rubbed my head and said "awww," but it didn't make my paw feel better. She played with my paw. A couple times it hurt, but I'm brave. Mama whined and the Vet whined back. She said, "No more high jumping. He's still a little puppy." I thought I was a big puppy! The Vet must have really big dudes, but I never saw them. She gave Mama some small treats in a bottle for me. Then we went home.

The treat was bad. Bad! Must be dried rat. Mama put peanut butter on it and made me eat it. She held my face until I did. My mouth drooled on the sides until the rat went down. Good thing there was peanut butter! I ate a lot of the disgusting treats. At least one a day for a long time. The Vet probably couldn't get other puppies to eat it so Mama took them. She made me eat it with peanut butter and cheese sometimes. Once I even got cream cheese. With strawberries! Yum! I liked that. A lot! But not the rat treats. The treat was so bad I forgot I had a sore leg. Bad!

❧ TIPS:

Find play groups for your puppy. He should be socialized early and often.

Your puppy's behaviors may change after his first year. Your dog may start to exhibit fearfulness or assertiveness that you didn't see early on. They are becoming adults and their carefree, trusting, love-everybody nature will change as they become more familiar with their world.

Be aware and curb undesired behaviors before they become problematic. What's cute as a puppy may not be cute when he's full-grown.

Give your dog a lot of exercise. Walks are great. Playing with a ball or Frisbee is another way of interacting and bonding with your dog.

How you play with your puppy is very important. Minimize how high you allow your puppy to jump. Puppy growth plates can be harmed during strenuous activities— even running, not just trauma.

Obedience School

We did a poor job of training Duffy ourselves so we decided to learn from a professional. We enrolled in obedience classes a few miles from our home. We had to cross the infamous intersection where the screaming and crying starts. Duffy didn't disappoint us. Same chorus, different verse. Different observers, same disapproving stares.

Bernard decided, "I'll sit in back with Duffy. You drive!" Duffy's screams hurt his ears. He hoped sitting next to him instead of in front would help.

We arrived at the park deafened, but relatively unscathed. Coincidentally, the trainer's name was Ginger. I wondered if Duffy made the connection. He didn't want anything to do with her.

Ginger had us meet and greet the other students inside a fenced-in basketball court. Duffy proceeded to assert his presence and terrorized a few of the smaller dogs. Inciting the trainer's ire was not the best way to introduce ourselves to the class.

The end of each class became Ginger's people-training time where we learned simple grooming techniques, dental hygiene, and other important tips. We barely heard any of her instructions because Duffy announced his displeasure at having to wait with another dose of high-pitched screams. Even positioning ourselves behind and away from the group, he managed to drown out Ginger's instructions so we could only guess at what she said.

Mama and Daddy said it was time to take me to school since they couldn't walk me very well. They were pretty slow and didn't know where to go. They needed to learn a lot so it might be a good thing. So we went to obedience school. Since my parents didn't know Obedience, it was up to me to teach them.

Bad news. They stuffed me in Trouble again. I was sure this was the end. I'm grown up now. Over 40 pounds. Mama said eight months old. I guess that's old. Daddy put my dress on and tied us in back. Mama drove this time, and I screamed all the way. Everybody was barking or screaming again. Especially when we stopped. Daddy growled something bad about stoplights, but I couldn't hear because I was screaming and my tongue was leaking. I didn't like Trouble. Car Pet won't play with me. Car Pet doesn't tell me where we're going. Car Pet must be afraid of Trouble. Mama and Daddy barked too, so they don't like Trouble either, but somehow we went.

We found a new park with strange dogs and humans. We all went inside a big crate. Big! It fit a kazillion dogs! At least ten. Mama said it was a basketball court. The teacher said we could play, but nobody wanted to play with me. They ran away crying or tried to bite me. Some humans said I'm cute, but some watched me like they wanted to eat me. One lady got mad because I almost bit her puppy on the butt to give it what for. Daddy taught me that. I still didn't know what for. Everybody ran around chasing me and barking. I made humans happy. That's what I'm here for. Hmmm. What for. That's what for! Now I get it. I'm important. I'm the king! I reminded them whenever I could. Daddy got mad when I did.

The human teaching the class was Ginger. She's mean too. I guess if you're named Ginger, you had to be mean. I stayed far so she couldn't bite me. She didn't like me because I made a lot of noise. I didn't like my dress. Daddy got me a new collar. He called it Choke Chain. That's why I'm choking. Daddy barked at me and pulled hard when I tried to get away. Ginger yelled, "Make him toe the line!" I don't get it. I was towing as hard as I could, but Daddy got mad when I did. When Mama took my dress, I didn't choke so much, but Daddy walked away and I wanted to go with him instead. Then Mama got mad and barked at me too. The only good thing was my treats. Not enough. I just wanted to go to my old park to play. Didn't choke so much. I gagged a lot here!

School was bad. We should've brought my stupid sister instead. Nobody knew how to walk. We walked in circles, and I had to sit a lot. I didn't like to sit if I could play. We did a lot of flybys and flybacks at obedience school. We went one way, turned around, and went back. Nobody knew where to go. I wished they would just follow me.

When we stopped walking in circles, Ginger barked orders to everybody. We puppies were bored, but they just sat. I guess they didn't like the flybys and flybacks as much as I did. I'm tough, but I'm happy because my neck isn't skinny anymore. Not choking either. I screamed and everybody got mad and barked at me again. Especially Ginger. Mama and Daddy told me "Be quiet!" Everybody wanted to hear Ginger bark. Not me. I'm done!

So we went home. Mama and Daddy were sad. I could feel it. I didn't know why they weren't happy to be home like me. My tongue was leaking, but the Car Pet doesn't mind. He still didn't talk to me. He's a funny pet. Must be a Poodle.

We kept going to school a long, long time. Long. Mama said six weeks, but I know better. Daddy said it was forever! He's right. That's a long, long time. Long. My parents didn't learn fast so we kept going. I screamed; they barked. We walked in circles and I gagged. Ginger barked and everybody listened but me. We'd go home and Mama and Daddy were sad. I guess they liked it better than me. I'd rather play, but nobody let me sniff their puppies. It's hard to be king when nobody wanted to be my friend.

Tattooing

Ginger said dogs often get lost or stolen. If they ended up in the shelters around town, there's a better chance of being reunited with their families if they had a tattoo that identified their owners. Microchips hadn't been invented yet. She was so convincing, we signed up to have Duffy tattooed with my driver's license number on his thigh.

When it was our turn, Bernard escorted Duffy into a classroom as I waited outside with the other dog owners. Duffy's fear of anything resembling a needle or the buzz of a bumble bee sent him into a full-fledged frenzy. Both Bernard and Ginger's husband held our now 45-pound dog on the table while Ginger performed her handiwork. After hearing what had occurred, I hoped we didn't scar Duffy mentally for life! It certainly left an indelible scar on my heart.

> Ginger told Daddy to bring me to a room. I was sure she was going to kill me. Ginger didn't like me and growled at me all the time. She told Daddy to put me upside down on the table and hold me down. I fought hard. Another human had to help Daddy. Ginger got a big Bumble Bee and stung me inside my leg. It hurt, but I wasn't going to cry. If she killed me now, I'm going dignified. I got tortured instead.
>
> My parents said this was my Eye-Dee so if I'm lost I can be found again. I don't know how I can be lost if I know where I am. My parents are so confused. First, they thought I was lost, and then I wasn't. My head hurt. My leg too. Not going to cry, though. Uh-uh. Brave.
>
> I couldn't understand why my parents let Ginger hurt me. I thought they loved me. They were so sad after I got my tattoo that I knew they were sorry. Daddy's heart hurt. Mama cried all the way home. I let her hug me, but she owed me cookies, big time!

Graduation

We didn't make significant strides in our training, even while practicing at home. Duffy's single-mindedness with the training and shrieking to and from class took its toll on us, but we wanted him to have socially acceptable behavior. It just didn't work out as we hoped. After six weeks of Duffy's raucous conduct, Ginger told us we had graduated and didn't need to come back.

At last, obedience school is over! Good! Ginger gave everybody a paper and said to come back next week for the new class. She told Mama and Daddy I'm good and don't have to come back anymore. See! I knew it! Nobody listened to me. I had a lot of smart things to say.

Mama and Daddy are sad. "I guess we're on our own," Daddy said. They did okay, but I'll have to keep working on them until they get it right. If I could just teach them to keep up, we wouldn't do so many flybys and flybacks and my neck wouldn't be skinny anymore. No gagging, either. It's hard when my parents aren't as smart as me. They should know by now. I'm a genius. They're slow. But I try. Try.

🐾 TIPS:

Verbal commands should not be shouted repeatedly. Your dog learns selective hearing just as we do.

At least one session of obedience is a must, regardless of the age of your dog. Some places offer puppy socialization classes as well. You'll learn with your dog and make a lot of new friends along the way.

If a practice doesn't feel right, don't do it. Tattooing was a primitive way of putting a permanent form of identification on a dog. It was also barbaric and painful. Microchips are the method used today. It's a good safeguard if your pet is lost, but even this is no guarantee that a shelter will look for the chip.

Broom Monster

Discipline at home was a challenge. Duffy's carefree demeanor made everything a game until he encountered the broom.

Bernard said, "That dog of yours makes yard work impossible!" Of course, Duffy was my dog whenever he misbehaved, which meant all the time.

I had to laugh because I saw what Duffy did to the pile of leaves Bernard had pulled together. Bernard had to rake the pile several times. Duffy continued to play, picking up a big branch and hitting Bernard hard as he ran by.

Bernard let out an angry howl as he chased Duffy with the broom. In a flash, I heard the doggie door bang loudly and Duffy was in the house looking for cover.

Bernard laughed really hard as he recounted the event. "Did you see him chop block me when I swept the patio? He made me so mad I swatted him on the butt when he ran by. You should've seen him run for cover!" Later, the mere sight of the broom sent Duffy scurrying into the house. It became a lifelong warning for Duffy. He knew he'd reached Bernard's limits when the broom appeared.

Daddy was playing with a new yard toy one day. I was helping. He said it was a rake for leaves. I liked leaves. They're my favorite! I liked the pillow Daddy made for me to jump on. My string toy was happy too. We jumped in and out a lot. A kazillion times. At least five. My string toy had fun getting the leaves to chase us. I was happy! My tongue was happy too. Jumping up and down. I found a stick and ran to the leaves! The stick hit Daddy. Daddy didn't like it. He got mad and pulled out a big weapon. At first I thought it was a new toy, but the weapon hit me! Daddy barked and growled at me too. He said he'd "take the broom to me." He chased me around the yard. That was fun, but Broom Monster was right behind. Daddy didn't take the broom to me. It jumped over Daddy and came all by itself! I didn't like Broom Monster! It ran faster than Daddy. Flying. Yike! Eeek! Whine! Scary! I dropped my stick and ran in the house. String toy can find his own way in!

I didn't see Broom Monster too much. Daddy had to growl real loud. That's when Broom Monster came out to give me "what for."

Broom Monster didn't hear unless Daddy growled real loud. No ears like mine. Good thing. Scary when it came out. I ran when I saw it. I know there's "hell to pay" without Daddy saying it.

❧ TIPS:

Training continues throughout your dog's life. Reinforce old skills and teach him new ones. Practice with treats and lots of praise.

Sometimes a dog's own perception of danger will teach a lesson faster than any other correction you can devise. Find an object or word that will get his attention to alter unacceptable behavior without traumatizing or hurting him.

First Friends

Fred

Duffy met his first friend shortly after I brought him home. Our neighbors had a Shetland Sheepdog named Fred. He was nine years old when Duffy arrived. We didn't realize our neighbors had a dog until he poked his nose through one of the slats of our fence where Duffy played. We'd slip him one of Duffy's treats if he came our way.

Bernard spent a lot of time outdoors and saw Duffy scratching vigorously after spending a few minutes near Fred. Duffy didn't get too many fleas because he was bathed regularly, but I managed to get one or two flea bites after his forays with Fred.

Nita, our neighbor, and Bernard spoke often so one day he approached her about Fred. "Nita, I think your dog may have fleas," he stated.

"I hadn't noticed," she replied. She brought Fred out for a closer look and fleas blanketed Bernard's pant legs after a few minutes standing near her dog.

Even she remarked, "Fred is *covered* with them! Oh, my! I didn't realize he had so many *fleas!*" She felt terrible about neglecting him.

She raised Fred from puppyhood. He was her baby until she had her boys. Fred lived outside because her husband said dogs didn't belong in the house. As her responsibilities for raising two young boys increased, all she managed to do for Fred was feed him and give him an occasional pat on the head. She worked late so she didn't play with him anymore. Realizing she neglected him so badly brought her to tears.

The next day, Nita loaded Fred into her car. After Bernard and Nita talked, she decided to have Fred groomed and examined by a vet. He came home with a new haircut and fresher outlook. Nita thanked Bernard for letting her know about Fred's condition. She never neglected him again.

Fred lived behind our gate. Daddy said he's a Sheltie. Don't know what that is, but he sounded like a dog. Smelled like one too, only stinky. Not like Jingles, but still stinky. He must be sick. He didn't get out much. Daddy said Fred's parents didn't have time for him. When he came to the fence to talk, his mouth smelled like bad food. Paws smelled stinky too, and I got itchy when I stayed too long. Daddy said Fred needed a bath.

Fred's bored all the time. Nothing to do. I listened, but not long. Itchy. I told him about eating trees and running around the yard with my toys. Lots of fun. He peeked through the fence, but wasn't interested. Fred's old. Mama said at least nine. He didn't like to run. He said his paws hurt.

Fred used to play ball like me a long time ago. Not anymore. Not since his mama had her own puppies. His mama used to take him out to see friends and they played a lot. He had nice baths too. He didn't like baths, but wouldn't fuss if she gave him a bath now. She used to hold him and kiss him sometimes. Not anymore. Lonely. He dreamed of the old days when he was the only puppy. Her other puppies needed his mama more, so he waited for his food and hoped for a pat on the head every day. Sometimes she forgot the pat, but the food was good.

I remembered old days too, even though there weren't that many yet. I didn't have to share anymore. I played a lot and ate plants all day. I loved to play. Except when Daddy chased me with Broom Monster. Afraid. Stayed far.

One day, Daddy went to see Fred in his back yard. He told Fred's mama he needs the broom. Broom? Maybe Daddy will give them Broom Monster. No luck. His mama promised to take him to the broom for a bath. Broom Monster never gave me a bath. Good thing! Scary.

Fred had lots of fleas. Daddy brought some home to share. Mama wasn't happy. We were all itchy that night. Jingles too. She left early. To give away her new fleas.

Next day, Fred went to the Vet and came back bald. I think they gave Fred's hair to Bob. He didn't look like himself. I had to check. Yep, it's Fred. Same old stinky breath. Now I get it. He got Groomed! So I guess Broom Monster stays with us. Too bad.

Fred was scared at the Vet. There was a noisy Bumble Bee that pulled all his hair out. Good thing the Vet held it back. He was afraid it was going to eat him too. A Bumble Bee?! Yike! He got a bath in a big bowl after the Bumble Bee ate his hair. Hope I don't meet that Bumble Bee! Fred said the towel was the best part. Warm. Fluffy. Then the Vet got a big, loud hose to blow his brains around. Rooo! The hose made him dry up. I know Hose! Daddy uses it in the yard. Only water comes out of ours. I better watch so it doesn't blow my brains around. Yip! Made his ears itchy too. The Vet had to dig around to put his brains back in place. Then they cut off his toes! Whine! Fred said he was afraid at first. Fought hard, but it didn't hurt too much. The Vet even checked under his rootie-toot. Only Fred has a tail so it's not really a rootie-toot like mine. I'm special. They pushed him around a lot, but he felt better after. He was happy when his mama came.

I yipped a lot that day. I listened to Fred a long time. Didn't get itchy this time. Fleas must have a new home. Fred was funny. He told a good story.

⊛ TIPS:

When you get your puppy or dog, be prepared for a lifetime commitment. Many dogs become backyard fixtures when their families tire of or don't have time for them.

If your dog needs to live outdoors, make sure he has a proper shelter and a bowl of clean water every day.

Take the time to play with your dog at least once a day. Mix play and training at first to make it fun.

There are many medications to help your dogs be flea, tick, and heartworm-free. Ask your vet what is available. Your dog doesn't need to suffer needlessly with infestations that may be spread into your home or make him sick.

Auntie Carolyn

Carolyn, a friend from work, enjoyed hearing about Duffy's escapades. She loved dogs and had one of her own many years earlier. Her animated Southern drawl was delightful to hear as she gushed and squealed over our beautiful Duffy. He found ways to appeal to the ladies and loved the attention she lavished on him. When Carolyn's mother came to town during the holidays, she doted over him as well. He was in heaven when they came to visit.

Auntie Carolyn was Mama's friend from work. She liked me a lot. Mama says humans who liked me were aunties and uncles. Don't have too many uncles, but Auntie Carolyn was special. She's nice. She brought me cookies. She talked funny. Mama said she had a drawl. Don't know what that is. Maybe she meant drool. I didn't see any when she talked. She must hide it when she does.

She doesn't get enough cookies. She's skinny like McKenzie, not like Rusty and Dusty the sausage terriers. Maybe she's a Greyhound too, but not gray. Mama said she's blonde. Blind? I think Mama tried to fool me. Auntie Carolyn could see okay to me.

Auntie Carolyn loved me and yipped a lot when I showed up. I thought she had a squeaky. Can't find it. I sniffed to check, but Mama said that's rude. Can't find it if I don't sniff, but I listened anyway. Maybe Auntie Carolyn has only one squeaky so she had to keep it safe.

Her mama Dot was nice too. She didn't bite me like Ginger, and she thought I was smart. She drooled too. We didn't see her too much. She lived far away. Far. In Miss-yippee. She brought presents when she came. I liked that.

Mama talked about Auntie Carolyn a lot. She said she's from the South. She says "y'all" all the time. I yowl too, but I didn't think I'm from the South. Didn't know South. I guess that's where my mom lived. Maybe I should teach Auntie Carolyn to howl and say Rooo! instead. She might not drool so much.

 TIPS:

Introduce your dog to your friends. Your dog needs to socialize with people too.

Correct unacceptable behavior immediately so everyone has a pleasant experience.

Chapter 6

Holidays and
Social Events

First Thanksgiving

I brought Duffy home a couple weeks before Thanksgiving. Bernard, our chief cook, made a wonderful turkey dinner with all the trimmings to celebrate the holiday. Duffy and Jingles watched Bernard intently as he prepared the turkey. Jingles knew she'd get her share and Duffy stood by, hoping he'd learn more about the feast. He took in every aroma with heightened enthusiasm.

Daddy played with something called Turkey all day. It looked like a big ball to me. Mama said Butterball. Must be Turkey's name. Jingles stayed around Daddy, so I did too.

Daddy hid stuff in a special Turkey place. Secret. Mama called it stuffing. I wanted to see, but I'm too small. I tried to jump up, but Mama growled and said "No!" Then Jingles ran out. Jingles stayed far when Mama's mad. Maybe she would stuff

Jingles too. I saw where Daddy stuffed Turkey. Uh-uh. Not me. I ran with Jingles.

Turkey smelled good, but Daddy put it in a box called Oven and it started smelling better. I think Turkey's name is Betterball! When Daddy took it out of the Oven, everybody came quick, even Jingles.

Mama let me sit by the begging table tonight. Daddy gave Jingles some Turkey in her secret room and Mama gave me some in my bowl. Yum! Turkey is good! Daddy had to hide Turkey's stuffing. Must be what he saved with his yard spoon. That's good too. We didn't have to share. Nobody knew where it hid.

Mama taught me how to eat with a fork. That's when the really good stuff came down. Mama said, "You have to learn not to beg at the table. No jumping or stealing food. That's uncouth." We practiced a lot. Especially at dinner time. I sat like a good boy and waited for food to come down. That was easy because I'm always a good boy. I learned about gourmet food that way.

My First Christmas

We had our first family gathering at Christmas. It was very special that year. My mother (Popo) flew in from Hawaii, and Bernard's mother, Jeanne (who Duffy would know as Gramee), and his sister, Charm, joined us for dinner on Christmas Eve. We bought a tree but didn't decorate or put gifts under it, fearing our little puppy would create a huge mess, or worse.

When my mother arrived, she laughed at Duffy's playful antics, but ended up chasing him out of her bedroom. "I can't unpack! He keeps jumping in my suitcase!"

Once my mother settled in, she entertained him in his own territory. They enjoyed getting acquainted on the sofa. We told Duffy his grandma's name was Popo. A few days later, he met Gramee and Charm.

On Christmas Eve, we all gathered at our house. Charm and I put the decorations on the tree as Bernard prepared dinner. Popo and Jeanne sat and talked. Jeanne and I would tease each other relentlessly so there was a lot of laughter when she was around. Jingles disappeared when she saw the crowd. She still didn't trust people. This influx of new bodies was too unnerving for her.

After we finished decorating and tucking the presents under the tree, Duffy went back to his new dog bed for a nap. Remarkably, he never touched any of the decorations or presents. Our fears were unfounded.

Everybody was happy. My grandma from Hawaii came and brought goodies for Mama and Daddy. Her name is Popo. She patted my head, but only gave me cookies we already had. I love cookies! Any cookies! Yum!

She brought stuff in two boxes. No toys. Or treats. Only for humans. Nothing for me. Her stuff smelled like flowers. She must live in the yard, but only with flowers. She had some treats that Mama liked, but nobody gave me any. Daddy said it was too stinky. Smelled good to me! Mama called it rice crackers. And old fruits. Mama said they're preserved. Looked old to me. Dried up! Popo even brought cuttlefish for Auntie Charm. It didn't look like it could cuddle anything. It looked dead. Like my string toy. It smelled good too, but I didn't get any of that either. Popo didn't like to share. I shared, but she didn't like my stuff.

Humans from Hawaii must like their food stinky. I want to go to Hawaii and get my own food. Hawaii must be far away. Way past our park!

Popo got to sit in Mama's seat on the sofa. She must be alpha dog. I liked my seat better. Nobody got my seat. Not even my stupid sister.

Daddy put a tree in the house. Maybe it was a puppy and needed company. Daddy had to put water in a big cup for it every night, but I think the tree was sad. Trees are supposed to be in the yard. Everybody knows that! It kept crying and little dry leaves fell on the house grass. I liked the tree and ate the bottom. It was good, but my face got stuck when I ate too much.

Gramee and Auntie Charm came over. Auntie Charm played with me and put toys on the tree. Mama said they were ornaments, but they looked like toys. Mama wouldn't let me have any. I got a big round pillow under the tree to lie on when Mama and Auntie Charm played with the tree. I could smell a tree inside my pillow. But it wasn't a tree. Daddy said it was bark, but I didn't hear it say anything. Must have quiet barks. I liked my pillow and ate a hole in it. Daddy wasn't happy because he got it from L.L. Bean. I never met L.L. Bean, but he gave me a big box for my pillow. I wondered if he had a puppy too? Maybe his puppy would play with me at the park. I looked inside the box, but Daddy took it away to play with later.

Popo and Gramee barked and yipped a long time. Boring. They must not have any toys. They could share mine. I tried. Daddy was busy with dinner, but not mine. I'm hungry, but nobody cared. My stupid sister disappeared. Smart. I ate my pillow until somebody fed me. Mama's always good for a cookie.

Everybody had a good smelly dinner but me. Mmmm! I sniffed at it a lot. No room at the begging table. Daddy tried to fool me with the same old stuff. He put tasty water called Gravy in my food and some meat they didn't want. It was good. Not enough. I sat looking at Mama with sad eyes, but everybody said, "Go away!" I tried to get on Mama's lap, but she barked and growled. Nothing to do but eat my pillow.

They said Santa was bringing something for me tomorrow. Don't know Santa, but he must be a nice dude. He should come tonight. He could give me some meat he didn't want. Later, Mama gave me more meat when nobody was looking. She called it steak. Sneak, sneak. Yum! I love steak! Betterball too, but steak's my favorite! I could eat it every day!

The next day, I got lots of new toys and treats. I got real nice toys from everybody. They said it was because of Christmas. I never found out who Christmas was, but I'm glad he thought of me. He sent Santa to bring it so my parents would play with me in the yard. Santa's a good boy, even though I never saw him. He's smart too. He knew what I liked. I got some new balls and squeaky toys. My squeaky doesn't squeak anymore. I guess I killed my squeaky. I got new treats too. Some I never ate before. Smelled like Popo's yard. Must be treats Popo forgot from Hawaii. Santa had to walk far for them. At least two blocks. I hope he comes again soon!

My First Party

Duffy went to his first birthday party at the park. It was Scarlett's fourth birthday. Judy, Scarlett's owner, brought party favors and treats for everyone to share. It was an impressive affair. Everyone received party hats. Several dogs wore their hats without a fuss. Duffy was busy getting into everyone's business so no hat for him. We had birthday cake and the dogs all received ice cream cups full of a treat called Frosty Paws. We'd never heard of it before, but the dogs loved it. We popped the frozen treat onto a paper plate and Duffy tried to swallow the treat whole. He didn't, but he ate it in three bites.

Even though Scarlett received the bulk of the gifts, Judy gave each of the dogs their own package to open. Duffy had a grand time and enjoyed his treat. We still remember that day fondly.

Scarlett's mama invited us to a birthday party at the park. It was my first party. I had fun! Nobody was mad at me for running over their puppies and we all had Frosty Paws to eat. Mama says it's doggie ice cream. Mmmm! I love ice cream! Everybody had one. We even got funny hats. I didn't like mine, but Daddy said I have to wear it to be polite. I don't know Polite, but I'd rather be me so I didn't wear my hat. Scarlett got some good toys and treats. Daddy said they're birthday presents. I hope I get a birthday party soon so I can get more toys and treats. I like presents. A lot!

Once we discovered where to purchase Frosty Paws, we made weekly trips to the grocery store to keep Duffy supplied. He now ate the treat from the cup so it would last longer than three seconds. Bernard wondered why Duffy didn't get brain freeze that first time.

Sometimes the store would run out of Frosty Paws for weeks! Since the treat became a nightly routine, I improvised by mixing some juice and skim milk together and freezing the concoction so Duffy wouldn't miss his nightly treat. We were slaves to a routine we created. Duffy sulked if we ran out of Frosty Paws.

My parents gave me Frosty Paws every night after that. They fixed something special if the Store gave too many away. I was real sad if I didn't get my treat. Yum! I love Frosty Paws. Mama tried to give me a cookie instead once and I spit it out because I was sad.

Mama taught me to "take the cup to the trash." I cleaned up good. I have couth.

When Mama and Daddy had friends over, I showed them how to "take the cup to the trash." I'm the only one who did it. They thought I was special. I made them laugh. Everybody yipped and barked when they watched me, but they left their stuff behind. I guess they didn't know how to clean up like me. I had to teach them so they could practice at home.

🐾 TIPS:

Teach your dog guest etiquette and table manners. The most basic rules would include no inappropriate jumping, barking, or sniffing. Stay away from the table or plates of food.

Practice before your guests arrive. He needs to obey the rules or be left out of the affair.

Dogs love presents. Include your dog in your gift giving. He'll learn to love opening his own presents.

When you start a daily routine or tradition, be prepared to stick with it. Your dog won't let you forget. Especially when food is involved.

Girl Scout Cookies

Jeanne loved Girl Scout cookies, but Girl Scouts were a rarity in Las Vegas. A friend's daughter belonged to the organization, so we had a willing supplier. We'd buy dozens of boxes and ship half of them to Jeanne. She was always happy to get her yearly allotment.

Daddy and Mama yipped a lot when a big box came. A girl brought it. Her mama too. They were nice. I didn't have to go to the yard to talk to myself. They let me stay and sniff the box. Nobody gave me those cookies. Mama said we're sending some to Gramee. My parents just didn't want to share. Sometimes Daddy said "Five-second rule" so I could have one of those cookies. Mama always said "Leave it!" Too late.

Easter

Our friends, Cindy and Ron, have a daughter named Tiffany. The five of us arranged to meet for Easter Brunch at a fancy hotel. As a surprise, I decided to create an Easter basket for her. She was five at the time and loved those baskets.

Bernard and I boiled a few eggs and dyed them. We'd purchased a chocolate bunny and other candies to add to the decorated basket. Duffy did his best to sniff everything before I placed the items in the basket. He ate one of the boiled eggs as his own Easter treat.

One day, Mama gave some eggs a bath in a big hot bowl. They didn't look like eggs when they came out. She said they were dyed. I'm glad I didn't die when I had my bath. Easter's eggs weren't so lucky. They must be weak. Every time Mama washed one, they died and looked funny. I ate one too, but I felt bad for Easter. Her eggs dried up when they died. Must be bad eggs.

Mama made Easter's basket and put her dead eggs inside. She put some toys with the dead eggs. Just like the Christmas tree, only these smelled good. Mama said "it's chocolate inside" and I couldn't have any because it's bad. Chocolate doesn't look bad, but maybe it's pretty outside and bad inside. She said Easter's Bunny would take them to Tiffany. Tiffany was somebody's puppy. She lived far away. Far. Where they liked dead eggs. Mama and Daddy put Easter's basket in Trouble to show Bunny where Tiffany lived. Oh, no! Trouble might take him to the Vet. No way to warn him. Too bad.

I wondered if Easter's Bunny delivered the bull terriers yet. They looked okay at the Vet. Not dead like Easter's eggs. Easter's eggs didn't have paws, so they didn't get around much. The bull terriers didn't have to sit in a basket. I hope they get delivered soon. Hard to live with egg for a face.

I wish I had my own Bunny. I tried to catch one in the yard, but he was too fast and too small. He ran under the gate before I could get him. I want to figure out how to make eggs. Then Mama might get me a Bunny for my own basket. I don't want my eggs to die, though. Mama might make me eat them.

Halloween

Duffy loved to greet trick-or-treaters with his famous howl. Not everyone appreciated his howl as much as I did, but his bowl-diving made everyone laugh. Not so for Bernard. It was a battle to give kids candy while trying to get Duffy's face out of the bowl.

> Mama and Daddy didn't like Halloween. Lots of puppies Daddy called kids came over. Daddy didn't want me to meet Kids. They tried to steal my candy. I howled when they did. Their parents got scared when I howled. I stuck my face in the bowl. Daddy got mad and barked at me. Then Mama would send me to my yard to talk to myself.

Carolyn's Wedding

Carolyn found a wonderful man. After a comfortable and cozy courtship, they decided to marry. Roy was several years older than Carolyn, but their bond and happiness with each other was evident. She'd been alone for a few years after her divorce, so we were pleased she found someone to share her life again.

Shortly after a visit to Las Vegas to see Jeanne and Charm, Carolyn and Roy got married.

> Mama and Daddy left me at home to get married. Auntie Carolyn and Uncle Roy said to come. I thought they meant me too, but no. I got left at home to suffer. With Jingles. Nobody asked me. I stayed home and starved. We waited and waited, but they were gone a long time. Nobody cared. They ate wedding cake too but didn't bring me any. I love cake! It's my favorite! I'm hurt. Rooo! What's Cake?

🐾 **TIPS:**

Chocolates are not good for dogs. Although some dogs can tolerate chocolate without getting sick, it's best not to get them used to the taste. Check with your vet for a list of toxic foods.

Teach your dog "leave it." It's important he understands there are things he should not have or ingest. Obeying this command will keep him out of harm's way.

Eggs can be a great treat for your dog. Cook the egg rather than serve it raw to your dog. Salmonella has been known to crop up in raw eggs.

Expose your puppy to children, but be sure the children are instructed on how to meet your dog first. Have them approach your dog slowly and offer a closed hand to sniff first. Pet him under his chin rather than the top of his head. Rushing up to a dog or trying to grab him around his neck may be an invitation to get nipped.

House Guests at Our New Home

I invited a couple of friends to visit with us after we moved to our new home. My classmate from high school, Tsuki, visited first. She and I renewed our friendship over the many trips I'd taken to Hawaii to visit my mother and later, other relatives. She helped me through many rough patches during my mother's final years. I was overjoyed she would be our first houseguest.

A few months later, my cousin Linda and her husband came for a visit. What a grand way to celebrate both Bernard's and Glenn's birthdays together. We decided to take them to a San Diego Chargers game. No professional football team resided in Hawaii, so we all looked forward to this event. After the game, Glenn didn't want the evening to end so we stopped for dinner on the way home. We left Duffy for many more hours than before. We didn't have a doggie door, but hoped he could hold on until we returned home.

Since we moved, I met new friends. Mama said they're from Hawaii. My Auntie Tsuki came first. Her bag smelled a little like Popo's, only different. She had a puppy named Pua. I didn't know they called dogs poor. Mama said I'd like her. Daddy said Pua's a pit bull and I might not. I looked for Pua, but she didn't come. I guess because she was poor. Auntie Tsuki's box had some of Pua's hair in it. She smelled nice. Too bad. I need a new friend. I missed my old friends.

Auntie Tsuki brought treats for me! Good girl. I liked her a lot. She knew how to make friends even though she didn't smell my butt. I tried to smell hers, but Mama said, "no." I sniffed when nobody was looking.

Our next visitors were Auntie Linda and Uncle Glenn. They didn't bring any cookies, but always brought home leftovers for me to eat. Mama said the food came in a doggie bag so I knew it was for me, but I didn't get much. Only one bite. Everybody liked my doggie bag, so they ate it. Why did I have to share my doggie bag? I shared, but nobody wanted my stuff.

One day they went out and left me alone with my stupid sister. All day! Jingles cries all the time now. Mama and Daddy were gone a long time! Long! All day! Auntie Linda and Uncle Glenn must be lost.

I had to pee, but being lost must be worse. Our house didn't have a doggie door for me. So I suffered. A lot. Maybe Mama and Daddy are lost! I hope not. I didn't want to panic. Maybe they're looking for my doggie bag. I hope they bring it soon. I'm hungry and nobody cares.

🐾 **TIPS:**

House guests make new demands on your dog. Being a positive integral part of the visit is important.

Be aware of your dog's needs as well as your guests' needs since this is a 24-hour experience for both.

Christmas at Our New Home

We invited several friends to our home for a Christmas party. We had our concerns about Duffy's behavior, but he managed to endear himself to our visitors and entertain them with his parlor tricks.

This Christmas was special for us. Bernard found a large tree for our living room. We decorated the tree and the staircase with every garland, ball, and string of lights we owned. I bought a couple of animal-themed Christmas stockings to hang from the banister and of course presents for Duffy and Jingles under the tree.

By now, Duffy was a master at opening his own gifts. We let him tackle his own packages first. Our friends left toys and treats for him too. His huge pile of gifts thrilled him, but he made sure he didn't miss anything when we opened ours.

Mama and Daddy invited some humans to visit. Mama called them Guests, but they looked like humans just the same. Uncle Al sat in Daddy's "hell to pay" chair. All night. Daddy didn't growl or bark. Uncle Al must be alpha dog. Small alpha dog. Like Rusty and Dusty the sausage terriers, only skinny and short. Like a Poodle.

Auntie Dot got to sit in Mama's chair. Everybody else sat on my sofa or at the begging table. Even the sofas in the living room. We had a big begging table now. Mama put lots of food on it, but I'm not allowed to beg there. Mama sat with me on the house grass. Jingles disappeared. Too much yipping and barking.

Humans brought me lots of presents. I could smell cookies and toys. Some in bags. Mama tried to hide them. Not fair. My stuff. She said I have to wait for Christmas. I wish he'd get here soon. Still don't know who he is. I'll even share! Maybe…not.

Mama said Santa's coming tonight. I remember him. He found me even when I wasn't home. He must be a genius too. I hope he finds us at our new house. Mama made me wear socks so everybody could laugh. Not funny, but I'm getting presents so it's okay.

We ate a lot tonight. Everybody gave me treats when nobody was looking. Sneak, sneak. I got Frosty Paws later. Nobody else. I ate it all. Empty cup. I showed them how to "take it to the trash." Everybody yipped and said I was smart. I'm good.

Christmas came early. I was still dreaming of the shrimp, chicken, steak, chips, and cookies I ate last night. Yum! We had presents by the tree. This tree didn't cry as much as my first one.

Brave. My parents let me open my own presents. I'm a big boy now. I know how. I had a kazillion presents. Lots of treats and toys. Santa's a good dude! Wish I knew where he lived.

🐾 TIPS:

Parties in your home can be lots of fun for your dog. Be sure your guests know what they can and can't give him. Too much of a good thing can cause indigestion, or worse.

Let your dog be part of your home gatherings. Be sure he knows the rules so everyone can have a good time.

Auntie Alma's Christmas Present

Alma, a dear friend, gave us a spectacular gift. She had a painting of Duffy commissioned to grace our home. Carol, the artist, created a rendition of Alma's dog, a golden retriever, and Alma loved the painting so much, she thought Duffy should be immortalized too.

Carol took several photos of Duffy one afternoon and the painting she created was a rendering of several of the photos she took that day.

My Auntie Alma said I'm a pretty boy! My parents said Alma gave us a portrait. Don't know what that is. Hope it's cookies. She said somebody was going to draw a picture of me for our new house. I guess our house needs an Eye-Dee so it won't get lost. My picture is good as any. Won't hurt like a tattoo!

A lady named Auntie Carol came over and took pictures of me being cute. She had cookies. I tried to help myself, but Mama grabbed the bag. She moved fast when it's food. Rations. Auntie Carol took a lot of pictures. Not enough cookies for all those pictures. I waited for her to draw on the house, but she went home instead. I have to watch the house myself so it doesn't get lost before we get our Eye-Dee.

One day a big picture came home with Mama and Daddy. Big. Mama and Daddy showed me. They yipped a lot. They said it was artwork. I looked for Art but didn't see him. He must've starved since he didn't get cookies for his work. I guess Auntie Carol forgot my cookies too. Daddy said the picture looked like the "hound from hell." I thought it looked like me. He gets confused. Still no cookies. I went back to my sofa. Boring.

Next day they put the picture on the wall. Now the house is safe.

❧ TIPS:

Commemorate and celebrate your dog in photos and videos. He will be in your life a short time, but memories are forever. It's never too early to take that photo!

Looking back at moments sometimes forgotten are the best keepsakes you can have of your special dog.

Chapter 7

Yard Duty

Vegetarian

Duffy's love of vegetation as a puppy amazed me. Nothing was sacred. He ate the long stalks of a poinsettia plant. We thought he'd poisoned himself. We called the vet, but she said to watch him and not let him eat more. It's not deadly, just sticky.

While Bernard cleared away the remaining stalks, Duffy discovered a six-foot long limb of a tree in the back corner of the yard. He tugged and pulled until he freed the branch from the rest of the wood pile. We had a very strong and determined puppy! He pranced around the yard with it before settling in to chew. Other times, he'd run with it, knocking over patio chairs and whatever else stood in his way.

His gnawing on vegetation helped ease his teething. By the time his adult teeth grew in, he'd destroyed the equivalent of a 25-foot tree. Although we had to be sure he wouldn't get sick from the plants, it certainly was a reasonable alternative to shoes, clothes, and other personal items.

Mama called me a vegetarian because I liked to chew all the stuff in the yard. Especially the poinsets. She worried they were poisonous. I don't get it. First, she said they're poinsets, and then they're poison. I liked them because they tasted good. It made my face sticky. That's not too bad unless the sticky got on my face. Then it hurt when I tried to bark. If I closed my mouth too long, it got stuck that way. Then it really hurt. I had to keep it moving. I tried to get cookies, but it didn't always work.

An old tree slept in the yard and I got lots of sticks to chew. Daddy said it was dead from termites. I'm glad I didn't have termites. I might be dead too. He laughed when I grabbed a big stick and ran around the yard. The stick was way bigger than me, but I was a strong puppy. Daddy told Mama, "The little critter pulled a huge branch out of the woodpile. It was six feet long!" I didn't see any feet on it. Must be small feet. It didn't last long, though. I chewed until the stick got real small and disappeared. It made my teeth happy because they hurt. Mama said, "Duffy's losing his baby teeth, thank God!" I guess that's a good thing. My teeth were okay, but better to lose them than my face. Yum! I liked trees. Not as much as cookies, though. Cookies are my favorite!

My parents watched me potty every day. Daddy said, "I can't keep track of what he puts in his mouth. He eats everything!" My rope toy came out once, but not the tree. I guess that's okay. Daddy picked up my rope poop with his yard spoon and threw it in a can to give to the neighbors. I never saw it again.

Yard-Proofing

Duffy enjoyed playing with everything in the yard. His intense focus on new sticks, plants, toys, and balls often caused him not see objects that were right in front of him. He bounced off the side of the house and fencing a couple of times. He also ran into the trunk of our orange tree. None of those bumps bothered him as he continued to play without a yelp or whimper.

We were concerned when he ran around the yard dragging those long tree limbs behind him. He missed one of our windows and several rose bushes, a few of which he tried to chew as well. Bernard put up bumper guards so Duffy, and our home, would avoid serious damage.

I liked playing in the yard with my parents a lot. My favorite! Especially with my toys. Sometimes we'd play real hard and I'd hit the house. Didn't hurt. Too busy playing. Daddy said I was "an accident waiting to happen." He bandaged plants called Roses to be sure they don't get hurt. They have Bumble Bees on them. Only their butts stick out. Daddy called them Thorns. They hid until you got close. Then they poked you. Sneaky. I didn't chew them like the other plants. Daddy would chase me with Broom Monster if I tried. He said I didn't have a lick of sense. I never licked Sense before, but not going to try with Broom Monster around. Scary.

Daddy put bandages near the windows too. He said, "Duffy, you never watch where you're going." I do, but I saw another dog near the window so I had to look. One time I got too close and the dog hit me in the nose. That dog played rough. Bad dog! I barked but he just stayed in the window and looked at me. I don't look at him anymore. Daddy said I might hit the house again, so the bandages are just in case. Our house lives In Case now so I didn't hit it anymore. Must hurt the house like the dog who hit my nose.

Spring Planting

Bernard enjoyed spring planting. With a young pup along, gardening became exasperating, but I found it laughable and entertaining. Bernard would dig a hole and carefully place the new shoot. Duffy followed behind and dug it out. Bernard threatened him by whacking the ground with his spade and Duffy backed away and howled with glee. This was his cue to "chase me!" He watched closely for the next plant to go in the hole, and then dug it out when Bernard turned to prepare the next hole. This went on for three or four tries before the infamous broom appeared. That was Duffy's cue to run for cover. The big bang of the doggie door heralded Duffy's return to the safe zone and the end of the game.

Daddy dug a hole in the yard. I tried to copy Daddy, but Mama said it's not allowed. So we dug a quiet hole. Daddy didn't dig enough when he stuffed the plant in. Parts were sticking out. I dug more and got barked at and chased around with the yard spoon. That was fun! I barked and ran. Daddy was mad. We were digging too loud. I didn't know how to dig a quiet hole.

I helped Daddy a lot that spring. He called it Gardening. He dug quiet holes, and I checked them out. He wouldn't let me help. He tried to whack me with the yard spoon a couple times but missed. Too fast. That was fun! Couldn't potty on his Gardening, though. He'd chase me with Broom Monster then. Scary! A lot of the Gardening got bigger because I wasn't loud. I guess that was okay. Daddy was happy. Mama too. I got a lot of new stuff to sniff and pee on. My private mail. Secret.

🐾 TIPS:

Be aware of toxic plants and foods that are harmful to your pet. Check with your vet as he can tell you about specific plants more common to your area.

Your dog will be happy to help with your gardening. Be prepared to spend a lot more time outside undoing his handiwork.

Peaches

Duffy never tired of gardening with Bernard. As he matured, he stopped digging up the plants, but this time Bernard planted a new tree. Duffy's run-ins with the broom taught him to listen for key words signaling what we expected of him.

The peach tree was off limits. Duffy understood Bernard's warning, "Don't touch!" when the tree was planted, but Duffy found ways to skirt around those instructions when it served his purpose. Because of his ingenuity, we never had a single ripe peach from that tree.

Daddy made a quiet hole and put a tree in it to grow termites. It didn't smell like the one I dragged around the yard, but he told me not to touch it or there's "hell to pay." I sniffed close, but didn't touch.

Mama said it's a peach tree. I ran around and checked it every day. It didn't smell like termites. I guess that's okay. Maybe the termites are small yet. I couldn't tell because it was in the quiet hole with "hell to pay."

I checked it out a lot when Daddy wasn't around. Sneak, sneak. Sometimes he chased me with Broom Monster if I got too close. I peed on it when Daddy wasn't looking so everybody would know it's my tree.

One day, it had puppies! Mama said they're peaches. "Don't touch the tree!"

The puppy peaches smelled nice. They didn't say don't touch Peaches. I ate them when nobody was looking. Daddy and Mama caught me once and laughed. "He's on his tiptoes!" They think I'm smart because I picked Peaches without touching the tree. Even from the top. Not going to touch the tree. Don't want Broom Monster to get me. Uh-uh. Not me. Scary!

Jingles and the Blue Jays

Jingles was an adult semi-feral cat when we first saw her. She'd been abandoned and wandered into our yard for refuge. She was very fearful of humans in general and hadn't allowed us near her for months. Bernard loved cats so he took his time to gain her confidence and when he did, she stayed for good.

Jingles hunted for her food even though we fed her regularly. Her prowess was remarkable, but blue jays got the better of her during fruit season. Duffy tried to fend them off when they pecked her.

Jingles played a game with birds. Sometimes they lost. Then Jingles had dinner.

Daddy said, "Don't tangle with the blue jays. They're mean."

It's hard to fight with blue jays. They fought back. They liked to poke heads. They made Jingles and Daddy mad, but not me. Jingles' head hurt from the pokes. She tried to fight back, but they were big and poked her a lot. She ran home to her little box when they did.

They tried to poke my head, but I'm too fast. I tried to catch them like my ball. Daddy ran inside when they tried to poke his head too. He's too big for the little box so he ran for his "hell to pay" chair.

I chased them away. I won't let them have my Peaches. I jumped and snapped at them when they tried. My tree. Mine! Only Mama and Daddy can have Peaches. They didn't eat them like me. They didn't like green. Too small to eat. They always came small. I stood up on my back paws and pulled them off. Mama barks at me when I do. "Not ripe," she says. I thought I got it right. So confused.

Next day, she checked my poop for pits. Don't know Pits. He must like poop.

Orange Treats

Duffy enjoyed playing with his toys in the yard. One day he discovered an orange under the tree and mistook the fruit for his ball. When he bit into it and discovered orange juice, he bit new ones daily until we finally stopped him. We didn't want the acid in the fruit to harm his teeth. Besides, we hoped to have a few oranges for ourselves since we didn't get any peaches.

Mama and Daddy liked to throw toys for me to chase in the yard. My favorite was my ball. I picked up a ball from under the tree. Daddy said that's not a toy. It's an orange. It didn't squeak, but still fun. Especially when it leaked. Good water. Yum! Mama said it's not good for my pearly whites.

I don't know Pearly Whites. Maybe they had allergies. I have allergies. Maybe they are allergies! Don't want to mess with allergies. Have to see the Vet. "No, no. Bad!" She'd shoot me then. I tried not to be a baby, but she made me cry. Undignified. Hurt my feelings. I have feelings everywhere. The Vet found them all the time. Daddy said I have to be a man and not wimp out. Easy for Daddy to say. The Vet never shot him!

Watermelon

Duffy was a watermelon fan from the moment he had his first taste. Fruit trucks used to make regular stops in our neighborhood and watermelon was my favorite. During watermelon season, I'd often buy a large one every two weeks. Duffy sat with his face in my lap, looking at me through his expressive brown eyes, hoping to get another piece of the sweet, juicy fruit. Sometimes he ate too much and suffered the consequences the next day. That never stopped him from begging for more.

Bernard created a mulch pile under our fruit trees. Banana peels, watermelon rinds, and other kinds of skins or shells would end up under the trees. Several weeks after our watermelon season, a sprig grew from this mulch pile. We thought we had a watermelon plant. We were surprised when this turned out to be something else.

I had my first watermelon when I was two. I love watermelon. It's wet, but didn't taste like cookies. It drooled in my mouth and all over my face. Mama gave me a lot once and Daddy said I got the watermelon blues. I didn't see any blue watermelon, but I spent a lot of time in the yard. A lot. My tummy sang a lot too. It made a sound like my mom. Grrrrrr!

When I got older, I could eat lots more watermelon and Mama let me eat from the watermelon bowl. Daddy called it Rind. I don't get it. It looked like a bowl to me. I ate so much my face got sticky. Mama wiped my face like I was a baby. Embarrassing. Daddy said, "A real man has stuff on his face all the time." Mama really wanted a girl.

Once we had a watermelon in the yard. Daddy said. It had a flower on its tail and grew a snake. Didn't know Snake, but that's what Daddy called it. The snake ran across the yard until Daddy wrapped it around our orange tree. Daddy kept saying the tree is orange. It really was green.

The Snake got longer. Then a watermelon grew on it. Daddy said it was my job to watch it. Every day I made sure it didn't escape. It had a dress on so I knew it wouldn't go far. It couldn't roll fast. Another watermelon grew, but it was small. I guess that was the runt. Just like me. This was my favorite one, though it didn't talk much. Just laid there. Nothing to say. I barked at it once, but it didn't want to play. Boring. I hope it's more fun when it's bigger.

The first watermelon grew big real fast. It was fat too. I thought it was going to pop. I would if I was that fat. Like Rusty the sausage terrier. Daddy took its dress off one day and brought it in the house. I saw him cut the watermelon. Eeek! That's my watermelon! I'm supposed to watch it!

Daddy howled when he looked inside. It must've hurt to cut it. He said it wasn't a watermelon after all. It was a pumpkin! Mama and Daddy laughed about it, but my pumpkin watermelon was dead anyway.

Sad. I went out to make sure my runt was still there. It was. I told it his brother was gone. It didn't say anything. Nothing. Didn't even whine. I guess it didn't understand. It's not smart like me. I'm a genius.

Later, Daddy took the snake and my watermelon runt out to live in a can. The dead one too. Just like my mom, I never saw them again. My watermelon didn't even say good-bye. I guess that's how it goes. Kidnapped by a can and nobody says good-bye.

Landscaping

We moved when Duffy was seven. Our new backyard was a mass of dirt and clay at our new home. We needed to get landscaping put in right away. Duffy tracked dirt or mud into the house every time he went out. The tedium of cleaning his feet after his forays outside gave us motivation to hire a landscaper. Although the landscaper promised the job would take a month, it sat for over three months. Finally, our desired bushes, plants, and sod arrived and our patio was completed.

Duffy tried to supervise, but Bernard wanted the landscaping done quickly and Duffy only got in the way. He spent many days in the house watching from the glass doors, barking orders of encouragement.

I had a brown yard for a long time. Long. At least two weeks. A man came over and marked all over the yard. He left a lot of junk mail. Daddy didn't let me sniff. He said it was spray paint. No messages. Daddy said he was marking a design for our new backyard. He came back later with some Mexicans. Daddy said. I liked Mexican, but they didn't look like food. They were humans. They made quiet holes. I wasn't allowed, but I barked anyway. The whole day. Nobody let me go out to see. It's my brown yard. They were here a lot. Every day. For a long time. Long. Daddy said, "Months!" Too long for me to count.

Lots of dudes came to dig in the yard. We had holes for a long time. Long. They said too much clay. Who's Clay? All I saw was dirt. And holes. I checked out the holes, but Daddy moved me away. I tried to show them how to dig. They didn't like my hole. They chased me away. They talked funny. Daddy said it's Spanish. They're Mexican. Don't know Spanish, but I love Mexican. Mmmm! My favorite! Especially the cheese! And pork! I went see them every day. Just In Case they had some.

Mama gave them plums. Yike! My plums! She said it was mine! I followed her out. Don't give away all the plums! My plums! They didn't eat everything. They left the pits so Mama didn't have to check. Embarrassing!

They didn't know how to plant either. All the tops stuck out. I tried to show them. Daddy got mad and put my dress on, and then locked me inside to talk to myself.

Daddy put my dress on and took me out on my estate later. I checked my brown yard that night. Mama fussed at me because my paws got brown too. My paws got washed in a big bowl. A lot. I was afraid I would die at first, or dry up, but I'm okay. I'm luckier than Easter's eggs.

I wished I had my oranges and peaches. They didn't make the trip when we moved. They got lost. It's hard to follow with short paws. Sad. My new yard didn't have trees. The new yard was bald. Only dirt. Daddy promised me trees. Still waiting.

One day, I got my green yard. And a new plum tree. Yippee! I can potty where I want and there's new doggie mail to read. It was like my old backyard now. I was still waiting for the wildlife to show up. Mama said we had lots. Coyotes were wildlife, but they're boring to me. Jingles went to see them, but they only gave her rats and bunnies to eat. Not going to their house.

Super Bowl Cherry Tree

While shopping at a garden store one day, we found a cherry tree for sale. We thought about planting another fruit tree in the yard besides the plum tree I wanted earlier. A cherry tree was rare in Southern California. We decided to buy the tree and see if it would thrive in our weather

Our cherry tree struggled to survive. We harvested one cherry the first year before Duffy ran into it while playing and snapped a root. Later, a gopher damaged more roots and the tree slowly died. I was disappointed at losing the only cherry tree in the neighborhood.

One day, Daddy brought home a new tree to grow termites. Only this one was a Cherry Tree. Mama said it's going in on Super Bowl Sunday. I was looking for the big bowl, but the tree got stuck in a noisy hole instead. Mama and Daddy were yipping and Mama even barked at the TV. We could hear her all the way to Hawaii. At least two blocks. She said it's football. Looked like a TV to me. I waited for cherries or termites to come out, but nothing happened. I guess they got lost. I never found the bowl.

We waited and waited, but no termites or cherries came. We waited a kazillion days. Long time. Long. Only one cherry showed up. Mama ate it. She didn't share with us. No termites. Only a gopher. It was almost Super Bowl time again. Maybe he found the bowl. He tried to move the tree. No luck. Daddy used his yard spoon, but couldn't find the gopher or the bowl. He put food down the hole. Daddy only found a sick gopher, no bowl. The big bowl was lost for good. Daddy hoped Jingles could do a better job, but she liked rats better.

 TIPS:

Dogs are omnivores. That means they enjoy fruits and vegetables as well as meat. Many of the new premium dog foods include fruits and vegetables in their foods.

Carrots and string beans are great alternatives to commercial dog treats, especially if your dog is overweight.

Chapter 8

Home Deliveries

For the Love of Mail

Duffy's daily routine was to terrorize the mail carrier, Mr. Reynolds. He quietly guarded the door when he heard him coming. As soon as the mail came through the slot in the door, Duffy lunged at it, and then barked and howled until the carrier's footsteps retreated.

Bernard said, "Duffy's bad enough now but when summer comes, we can't keep the door closed. We need to get a mailbox and a security door." Bernard shopped for both items and installed them before summer arrived.

This worked out well because we started getting UPS packages from Bernard's mother. When she moved to Las Vegas, we traded several gift packages a year. Duffy's lunges at the door caused the UPS driver to drop our boxes several times as he scurried back to his truck. Mr. Reynolds endured Duffy's bluster daily, but his door lunges were very unsettling. Eventually, Duffy learned to accept our mail carrier, but he enjoyed inspecting the parcels and mail we received most of all.

My favorite time of day was when we got boxes from a truck. The boxes are from UPS. I could hear the UPS truck because it made a lot of noise. For miles and miles! At least two blocks. Daddy calls the human Mr. Brown. He liked to make me bark because he rang a bell. He dropped the box and ran before Daddy could open the door. I wanted to see who it was. Daddy's slow. Daddy and I would fight to get the box. Gramee sent cookies a lot. My favorite! I always got to taste them. Daddy said they're smashed because of me. I like smashed cookies because there's lots of crumbs. More for me.

Mr. Reynolds dropped and ran too. He used to push stuff through the doggie window in front, but Daddy put a new box outside the door. He wanted to get the mail first. Daddy said, "You make the mail soggy!" Not fair.

Mr. Reynolds liked to make me bark. I could hear him coming, but he didn't have a truck. He made a lot of noise in the box so I could bark. It's fun. Daddy growled at me to be quiet, and we fought to see who got to the box first. I got by sometimes, but Daddy's a big dude so he blocked the way most of the time. I couldn't reach the box so the mail didn't get soggy anymore. Mr. Reynolds didn't run fast like Mr. Brown. He's old! At least ten.

I liked my own mail. I had to go find it, but at least I had it all to myself. My parents let me read in private. No peeking. Secret. I learned a lot that way. More than them.

🐾 **TIPS:**

Introduce your puppy to regular delivery couriers in your neighborhood. Mail carriers are the ones who suffer the most when it comes to uncontrolled dogs, even behind secure doors. They will be seen as intruders until you take this one step. It will save you and the carriers a lot of stress, or worse, when they come to your door.

Chapter 9

Wildlife

The Skunk

Duffy ran into a nocturnal visitor prowling our back yard early one morning. He decided to greet the waddling black and white creature up close. Imagine our horror when Duffy slammed back through the doggie door, rubbing his face and chest all over the furniture and bed! We tried to keep him out to fend off the obnoxious odor, but he managed to rub himself everywhere in the house. His woeful attempt to escape the skunk's scent was sad to behold.

Bernard tried to grab him, but Duffy eluded us for seemingly an eternity before we could shove him out the door. It was nearly dawn by then, but not soon enough for stores to open. We desperately needed something to help us get rid of the smell!

The odor in the house dissipated after a few days of spraying and cleaning, but Duffy's chest was discolored by the skunk's spray, and the smell returned with every bath. I finally decided to cut away the yellowed fur. That finally did the trick.

One night, I went outside to pee and saw a stinky cat looking at my toys. I went to see. The cat turned upside down and peed all over my face. It burned, and I smelled real bad. Real bad. Really, really bad. I ran inside and cried. Daddy came out first and said, "Oh, Lord! A skunk!" He chased me around. Tried to catch me. I rubbed my face every place. Even on his "hell to pay" chair. I ran to the bed and rubbed on Mama too. Mama howled, *"What is that smell?!"* and said I was banished! I thought I got peed on, but Mama said it was Banish. I didn't like Banish. Not going to sniff that smelly cat again. Tried to make friends and it peed on me. Bad Banish. I rubbed my face on the grass. My eyes hurt. Stayed stinky. Long time. Long! Forever!

Daddy found "thank heaven for Nature's Miracle" and put some on me. Still stinky. Mama put some red water on me. She said it was tomato juice. Tasted good, but I was still stinky. Daddy escaped in the car, but came back with more stuff. I guess he felt bad that I'm stinky. They said I reek. Yeah, I was weak from the stinky, burny pee. I got a kazillion baths that day. At least four. They didn't give Banish a bath. He smelled worse than me. He ran away before Daddy could catch him. Even my stupid sister stayed away. She knew I was weak. Embarrassing! Can't be king if I'm weak. Not fair! I cried a lot that day.

Daddy found stuff to spray on the chair, but it wasn't so good. I could smell Banish forever. I kept my eyes open now when I went out the doggie door. Banish might still be there. I could back up fast if I kept one paw inside. Banish was mean! Even Gingers aren't that mean! I hoped he wasn't mean to my toys. I sniffed them. They're okay. They laid there without squeaking, so Banish left them alone. Mama said we got wildlife here. My life was pretty wild after I met Banish. Not playing with Banish anymore. He can have my toys next time he comes around.

🐾 **TIP:**

There is nothing worse than having your dog "skunked." A friend gave me this recipe to wash my dog. Luckily, I've never had to use it, but I would love to hear if this works.

Use this recipe FIRST before shampooing your dog.

1 pint hydrogen peroxide

¼ cup baking soda

Squirt of dishwashing liquid

This recipe is enough for two small dogs. Be careful not to get it in their eyes.

Jingles' Bunny

After our move, having Jingles indoors became an annoyance. She was still semi-feral so she yowled incessantly for her freedom. The wildlife inhabiting the canyons eagerly preyed on small animals left out at night. We were afraid she would be an easy target.

After months of sleepless nights, Bernard said, "It's time for us to let her out. We can't go on like this." He didn't want to do it, but couldn't take the yowling anymore.

Jingles found her own way out and didn't return for several days. We worried about her, but one day we heard meowing near a new home site. Her cry was unmistakable. After that, we let her come and go as she pleased. We hoped she could find safety and shelter on her own. It became obvious she preferred hunting for her own food.

Daddy finally let Jingles out. She made so much noise that Mama said he got fed up. I didn't see what he fed up on. I looked but couldn't find anything new to eat. Mama said there's too much wildlife for Jingles, but it was time to let her go. She made it home okay so I guess it wasn't as wild as they thought.

She was gone four days. Mama said. They thought Coyotes ate her. They made lots of noise at night. They had a lot of parties.

Jingles came back with rat breath. I guess they shared their rats with her. Coyotes didn't eat as good as us.

My stupid sister brought home a bunny one morning. I hoped it wasn't Easter's bunny. She'd be sad. It looked like a big, long rat. Maybe our neighbor Coyotes gave it to her. Daddy saw it in the yard. He told Mama only the ears and paws were left. Daddy picked up the stuffing with the yard spoon, but left the rest to lie around like my toys. My stupid sister and Daddy could play with them later.

When we went back out to look for Jingles' toys, they were gone. Daddy said she ate it. My stupid sister didn't share. That's okay. She eats pretty bad. She didn't hang around with us even when she had gourmet food. I told you she's stupid.

🐾 TIPS:

Be aware of the wildlife in your area. Small domestic animals are easy targets for coyotes and birds of prey. Check with your vet to see what precautions you need to take to keep your pet safe.

Snake bites can be lethal to dogs. Small rodents attract snakes. There are vaccines you can give your dog that can delay the effects of a snake bite. Talk to your vet about this.

Snake aversion training is also available, but it's not for every dog. Assess the practicality of this experience for your dog before you subject him to this training.

Boarding

Gordon Setters

Bernard and I made our first trip away from home shortly after we started Duffy's obedience lessons. Our instructor, Ginger, referred us to a woman who could watch Duffy at her home. She had two well-behaved Gordon Setters and felt Duffy might learn a few things during his stay. We were encouraged by Ginger's comments and decided this would be the perfect place to leave him for a few days.

When I was a puppy, Mama and Daddy had to go hunting. In Hawaii. Bad Ginger said a lady could keep me. I thought Mama and Daddy were doing a good job. Now, somebody else was going to take me. I don't get it. Didn't my parents want me anymore? I'm a good boy!

My parents stopped at a house with two big dogs. They wore curtains all the time. Daddy said they had real long coats, but I knew they were curtains. I played with curtains at my mom's house. I know curtains when I see them. Mama told me they were Gordon Setters. They didn't sit a whole lot, though. Only when cookies came. I know that job. Because I'm smart. The lady said.

I stayed there for a long time. Long. Forever! Five days. Nobody came for me. I thought Mama and Daddy got lost or didn't want me anymore. I was sad. Gordon and Setter played with me. We had fun. Then I remembered my parents and got sad again. Until dinner time.

The human didn't let me sleep on the bed. She stuffed me in a crate. I didn't cry, though. Not long. Gordon and Setter slept in crates too. They didn't get it too good here. Cheap cookies too. Not many. I didn't get what they got. She told me puppies didn't get big cookies. I think she's cheap. I waited and waited for my mama and daddy. They gave me lots of good cookies.

One day they appeared. Yippee! I was happy! My butt shook so hard my rootie-toot was looking at my face. I jumped and ran around for a long time. At least ten minutes. Mama said, "Look at my hula boy!" She was so happy to see me. Daddy too. No more cheap cookies! No more crate! Saved! Rooo! I hoped my string toy and sofa waited for me to come home.

They stuffed me in Trouble again. This time I was happy to go. I made lots of squeaky noises, but my parents didn't care much. I got to sit in back with Mama. I had my dress on, but Mama didn't have to pull hard to make me sit. I got to lie near my mama again. She kissed me and hugged me hard, but I didn't fight. I was so happy, my tongue leaked on the Car Pet. It still didn't care. It must be a Poodle.

Second Christmas

This year, my mother flew from Hawaii and spent a few days with us before we left for Las Vegas. Bernard's mother and sister moved there a few months earlier and wanted us to see their new house. The dog sitter wouldn't take Duffy again because he was so hyperactive and more than she could handle.

We reluctantly boarded Duffy at the vet so we could visit Bernard's family. We left Duffy the day before Christmas and returned for him first thing the morning after the holiday.

Duffy looked so downtrodden when they brought him to us. I was guilt-ridden for leaving him over the holidays. To make matters worse, the vet informed us that she now had to treat him for kennel cough because they unknowingly boarded a dog that had the disease. Even though he'd been vaccinated, they had to treat Duffy to be safe. My poor baby! How could I not feel ashamed for leaving him there!

His spirits lifted when he came home to a pile of his own Christmas presents. He was overjoyed at the new toys and treats he received, but couldn't understand why he didn't get to go on his walks for the next couple of weeks.

Popo from Hawaii came for Christmas. Then they all left me at the Vet. Gramee moved to Las Vegas and wanted everybody to come for Christmas there. I thought me too, but no. I was sad. All alone. I was scared. I cried a lot. Santa won't find me if I'm not home, and I wanted my presents! Waah! Rooo! I thought they didn't love me anymore and left me to rot with a sick dog. I cried when the Vet came, but they only played with me a little and fed me cheap rations. I didn't have my favorite ball, and the other dog kept coughing. Nobody else was there. Not even my stupid sister. Everybody was home eating turkey and steak but me. I love turkey. And steak. They're my favorite! I stayed there a long time. Long. Nobody played with me. Nobody gave me a cookie before I went to sleep. Or Frosty Paws. My heart hurt. I was all alone. No Mama. No Daddy. For a long time. Long. Except for the sick dog.

Lots of humans came the next morning. I hoped my parents would too. I missed my mama and daddy. And my bed. And my food. And cookies. And toys. And yard. And mail. And Jingles. No. Yes. They finally came and I howled with joy. I thought they left me for good, but they said it was only two days. Mama was real happy to see me. Daddy too, but not like Mama. We all howled and

I jumped a lot. And licked everybody. Except the sick dog. And the Vet. They were mean. I cried and nobody cared.

The Vet gave my parents some bad news. They said the other dog in the kennel had a cough. I knew that! Took only one cough for me to know. Because I'm smart. It took the Vet two days! I told them he was sick, but nobody listened. She said they had to treat me for kennel cough. I don't get it. The Vet gave me *bad* treats! The other dog was sick and I got the bad treat. I didn't want it, but ate it anyway. I just wanted to go home. I didn't care if I had to ride in Trouble again. The Car Pet was nice enough.

I got lots of presents when I got home. Santa came! I played all day long. Because of Christmas. I liked him a lot even though I never met him. Or Santa. My parents had fun playing ball with me, and I got a lot of squeaky toys and bones. Cookies too. I got a big rope toy. Big! It had strings. I liked chewing it. I shook it, but it hit me back. Hard. Not my friend. Stayed far. Long time. Long. Then I ate it. I got to chew and chew on all my favorite things. My squeakies died and lots of stuffing came out, but the toys were still good. Flat but good.

Jingles was happy to see us too. She didn't eat so good either. I told her about my rations. She listened but didn't feel bad for me. I guess her rations were worse than mine. She had rat breath again. Ewww! Disgusting.

I wanted to go out to the park. Daddy and Mama said no park because I had a cough. I think they're confused. The sick dog had a cough. I felt good. Still no park. No flybys. No mail. No friends to roll. And I kept getting the bad treats! The Vet couldn't give them away to anybody else so she made Mama and Daddy take them home. I had to stay home for a long time. Mama said, "Two weeks!" Just in case. I guess our house is In Case again because I can't go out. Daddy told Mama, "We're in for it now." That's because we're In Case. I didn't think it was too bad, but my parents ran away a lot. They called it Time-Out. That's okay. I had my toys and chewies. And I slept where I wanted. Not at the Vet's house with a sick dog. Daddy promised, "We'll never travel without you again." He kept that promise. Good.

🐾 TIPS:

When boarding your pet, take him to the facility to familiarize him with the site and staff first. Some dogs adjust well. Others may not and new, undesirable behaviors could appear from the experience.

Bring familiar toys, treats, and food when you board your pet. Most establishments will give you a list of items you can bring to ease his adjustment away from home.

Discuss how much playtime your dog will receive during his stay. Exercise is key to relieving his stress and boredom.

If your dog is most comfortable in your home, think of hiring a dog sitter to stay with your dog or drop by periodically to exercise him when you're away.

Grandmothers

Popo

My mother lived alone in our family home for many years. Access to and from the house was difficult for her. There were two flights of stairs between the house and garage. She managed well enough, but one day she fell in the house and no one knew. Her friend found her two days later, dehydrated but well enough not to be hospitalized. After this incident, we decided she needed twenty-four hour care. My trip back to Hawaii was a necessary, but unpleasant one to find a place for her in a nursing home. Bernard had Duffy all to himself while I helped my mother.

When I returned, my mother and I talked over the phone often. She voiced her unhappiness about her situation but managed to be stoic about it. She laughed when I told her Duffy looked for her in our guest bedroom when she called. She was never one to have a pet of her own, but she enjoyed Duffy's antics when she visited us.

Popo from Hawaii didn't come to visit anymore. She got sick and Mama had to put her in a home. She's lucky. Now she has a bed. She lived in a flower yard before. That's why she liked her bed here. She spent a lot of time in it. Daddy cooked chicken soup for her just the way she liked when she was here. She didn't eat it all so I got the leftovers. Yum! My favorite!

Mama would go visit Popo sometimes. Daddy said she had to fly to Hawaii. It must be a long way. At least two blocks. I wish they would let me fly. I only got to fly by. And fly back. Mama must be part bird. She never flew here. She might scare the crows. Daddy said she had to fly over the ocean. He told me it's water. Rooo! I can't fly over two blocks of water! I wish I could see Mama do it.

Mama talked to Popo a lot, but I don't know how. She calls it the Phone. I could hear Popo, but she wasn't here. Once she said, "Hi, Duffy!" I screamed and ran to see if she was hiding in the bedroom. Everybody laughed. I don't get it. When the phone barked, Popo, or somebody else, would show up. I still don't know where they hide. I looked but couldn't find them. I asked Jingles, but she just looked at me. Stupid. Daddy says, "Jingles' lights are on but nobody's home." We're home, but I guess she's not. Even if she's here. Just like Popo.

Losing Popo

After a short confinement in the nursing home, my mother made a dramatic recovery and returned home. She thrived with the company of a full-time caregiver and relatives providing 24-hour companionship.

A few years later, we discovered she needed surgery. Her doctor admitted her into the hospital for tests. She was upbeat when she called to tell me the results of her physical. Within a couple of days, everything changed. The surgeon visited her and told her very bluntly she had cancer. She never liked doctors or hospitals and this frightened her so much, she stopped eating and refused to abide by the doctor's orders. By the time I flew to Hawaii, the hospital moved her to ICU. A few days later, she passed away. What started out as a short trip became a month-long ordeal. Making arrangements for her funeral and giving away everything salvageable. Cleaning up her house before putting it up for sale took an additional three weeks.

Bernard's support was remarkable at this tragic time. "Take all the time you need. The office will survive without you. Duffy and I will be okay." Our daily conversations on the phone eased the pain of loss and separation. Losing my mother was sad, but I missed Bernard and my precious Duffy. Bernard said Duffy heard my voice over the phone and dashed from room to room looking for me. It made me miss him that much more.

Mama had to fly to Hawaii and was gone so long that I thought she was lost. I wanted to go find her, but I couldn't fly. I missed her. A lot. Cheap treats when she's not home. Rations! Daddy missed her too. He's happy when the phone barks. I heard my mama then. I ran around to see where she was hiding. I couldn't find her. Sad.

Daddy said we lost Popo. Someone stole her like my first sister. She had a new home because she's old and slow. I missed my Popo even though she didn't bring me treats. She sent toys sometimes. No more toys now. Waah! Rooo!

Mama came home and she was sad. I guess Popo was lost for good. Kidnapped. Nobody saw. Mama looked for Popo a long time. She was gone forever! Daddy said a whole month! That's way longer than a week. I won't ever get lost. I don't want Mama to be so sad. I guess that's how my mom felt when I got kidnapped. I wished I could tell her I have a good home. She would be happy to know.

One day we got a big box from Hawaii. Mr. Brown brought it. He's our UPS drop-and-run man. Only this time, the box was so big he couldn't drop or run. Daddy had to help him. Daddy pushed me inside. He said I was a nuisance. No, the box had new scents. I smelled the same.

It was Popo! Maybe Popo wasn't lost after all! I smelled her inside. Maybe she was too tired to fly so they sent her in a box. No. It was just her stuff. Mama marked her smell in the house so Popo could find us when she's not lost. Mama felt better after she put Popo's stuff around the house. I kept hoping there was something for me. Nothing. Too bad. Daddy didn't get anything either. Just the stuff around the house.

Gramee

A few years later, Bernard received a call from his mother. She told him the doctors found cancer in her lung. This was the first of two bouts of lung cancer she endured. She vowed to fight the disease and remained cheerful most of the time, even though the treatments wore her out. She had a raucous sense of humor, so I started writing letters from Duffy to her to keep her spirits up.

Mama said Gramee got lung cancer. Don't know Lung Cancer, but it made Daddy sad. Gramee had to go to the Vet to get shot. I hope they didn't send Ginger or the Bumble Bee.

Auntie Charm said Gramee came home. She stayed at the Vet for a long time. Long. At least two days. Mama sent Gramee some mail from me to make her feel better.

Dear Gramee,

I heard you're home at last! I bet you love sleeping in your own bed again. I love my bed. Especially when I get it all to myself. I lie upside down under the fan and let my tongue hang out to get cool.

Auntie Dot hurt her paw and doesn't feel good. I told her you're all fixed up. Maybe she should see your vet.

I hope you come see us soon. You can bring presents if you like. I like presents. Toys. And treats. And smashed cookies! Yum! My favorite!

Love your grandson Duffy

Jeanne called to say how much she enjoyed Duffy's first letter. The note was short but humorous. We'd send her a few more notes now and then. A funny anecdote or observation appeared in each one. She looked forward to those letters and we didn't want to disappoint her so I sent them as often as I could.

Gramee liked my mail. She told Mama and Daddy she laughed when she got it. I made her happy.

Mama wrote Gramee a lot after that. Because I know she liked my mail. My Auntie Charm went to school now. She wanted to nurse Gramee. My mom knew how. She should ask her.

Dear Gramee,

Daddy said you're home now but still sick.

Hope Auntie Charm does better in school than my parents when I was a puppy. They got kicked out. Daddy said I made too much noise. I had a lot to say. We had to ride in Trouble to go. I screamed for help all the way, but humans just looked at me.

The other dogs didn't like me because I was pretty. And smart. Mama said I was a nuisance. I don't get it. Everybody smelled new.

Mama's not too smart. Maybe she should go to school again.

Love your grandson Duffy

Visit to Las Vegas

Carolyn, her mother, and I planned a trip to Las Vegas to visit Charm and Jeanne. Jeanne's cancer was in remission then so we enjoyed being out and about together. Bernard, ever stalwart, stayed home with Duffy. We didn't ever want to chance another mishap with a dog sitter or boarding kennel. The stays only seemed to upset Duffy. We didn't trust anyone to care for him anymore.

"You ladies have a good time," Bernard said. "I can talk to Mom on the phone." I knew he was happy to stay. The thought of spending three days with five chatty women was too overwhelming for him. It was a great visit and the last time I'd see her.

Mama and Auntie Carolyn went to visit Gramee and Auntie Charm in Las Vegas. I didn't get to go. Daddy stayed home, but we didn't eat good. He said we're on rations again. That means nothing from the begging table. I miss my mama. She always made me practice with my fork. I liked that.

Everybody forgot my birthday too. Hunting must be bad in Las Vegas.

Gramee Gets Sick Again

Bernard and I were distraught to hear Jeanne's cancer returned. She didn't want to go through another surgery, but felt she didn't have a choice. The surgery took an immense toll on her body. Her diminished lung capacity forced her to use oxygen to help her breathe. She remained as positive as she could in the months ahead, but we knew inevitably the cancer would win this battle.

Gramee had to see the Vet again. She stayed a long time. Long. At least a week. We waited for the phone to bark. Auntie Charm was in there. I hoped she didn't get lost. I wouldn't know how to find her if she did.

Dear Gramee,

I heard you had to stay at the Vet's house because of surgery. I had surgery. I hope they put all your stuffing back. Did the Bumble Bee shoot you? I hope you didn't cry if he did. Have to be brave like me.

I could hear Auntie Charm whining but couldn't see her. Everybody's sad. Her heart hurt. I could tell. Daddy told Mama Cancer came back. Where did he go? I thought he was with you. I guess Cancer's not a very good friend if he makes everybody sad. Tell him to go away again. If he does, maybe you can make me your smashed cookies again. Mmmm! I love smashed cookies.

Love your grandson Duffy

Gramee's Gone

The last report on Jeanne's condition came all too soon. Charm called to tell us she passed away. The finality of her death struck us hard. Our funny, cheerful matriarch was gone. We told Duffy his Gramee couldn't send him cookies anymore. I wasn't sure if it was my imagination, but he looked crestfallen too.

Auntie Charm whined on the phone one day. She said Gramee's gone. I guess that means she's lost. We still haven't found Popo. She must be looking for her. Now both of them are lost. When you're old, you get lost a lot. Sometimes forever.

Auntie Charm was real sad. She cried a lot. I could hear her say lost and sick with Cancer. Didn't know Cancer, but at least Gramee had company when she was sick. I hope Cancer was good to her before she got lost. He left but came back. Maybe he's helping her find Popo. Lots of crying and whining. Auntie Charm missed Gramee. Mama and Daddy missed her too. They used to laugh a lot when Gramee barked on the phone. Daddy said, "It was funny when Mama and Gramee called each other names." I thought they already had one, but maybe they needed more. Daddy's sad too but strong. No whining or crying. Alpha dog. Brave.

Auntie Charm didn't want Gramee to go, but Gramee left anyway. Now she's lost.

I hoped they'd find Gramee soon. I missed my smashed cookies. She didn't send them for a long time. Long. If Gramee finds Popo, maybe we'll get more stinky fish from Hawaii too. Jingles liked that.

🐾 TIPS:

Pets grieve too. Your dog may not have the same conceptual understanding of death, but he will know when a loved one is no longer available in his life.

Include your pet in your circle when you are grieving. He will be a tremendous comfort to you.

Chapter 12

Car Trouble

New Rides, New World

After years of listening to Duffy scream during our trips to the vet, I felt we should take him on a few fun trips in the car. Bernard didn't want to subject himself to more migraines, so I started venturing out with Duffy on my own. Even with Bernard's doubts, I still hoped I could someday ease Duffy's fear of car rides. We bought a harness so I could secure him to the passenger seat while I drove.

We took short trips around the block before venturing through the neighborhood. He started to see the car wasn't a bad place unless I did something out of the ordinary. He had an uncanny way of sensing my thoughts and feelings, and reacted as you'd expect on those occasions.

Mama took me for rides in Trouble when I got older. She told Daddy that I screamed and cried because I only rode to the Vet. No. It's because the Vet didn't like me. Every time we went, the

Vet shot me. With the Bumble Bee. I tried to stand my ground, but my butt brakes never worked.

Mama said I needed to see fun places in the car. So I wouldn't scream and cry and make Daddy bark at me. I had lots of fun places already, but Mama wanted to show me more. Trouble grumbled all the time. He doesn't like fun.

I could get in without my dress. Mama let me sit in front with my bandages. She called it Harness. Same thing. Still tied up. I have my own "hell to pay" chair now.

I sat in front for the first time. Daddy didn't want to go. He and my stupid sister went to hunt rats instead. Not my favorite. Mama's either.

It was different sitting in front. I got to stick my nose out and lick the air. I liked that. We went far. We rode at least five minutes. Sometimes we drove by the park and I stuck my tongue out to say hi. Mama talked to me the whole time. I wasn't scared that day. Brave. No screaming or crying.

One time, we got lost. I could tell. Bad Trouble. Not listening to Mama. Probably because it didn't have a dress. Mama was going in circles and her heart was running. I got scared too. She said she was lost. She wasn't mad at me, but I was scared anyway. I shook all over and cried. Trouble stopped and she hugged me for a long time. Long. I wanted to be brave, but I hugged back. Mama kept saying, "It's okay, baby boy. It's okay," until I stopped shaking. I love my mama. I'd miss her if she got lost.

We got home okay. I was happy to see my toys and blanket. Not going anywhere again. Uh-uh. Not me.

Fun Trips to the Pet Store

I tried to convince Bernard that Duffy was starting to calm down on our fun rides. Bernard had his fill of any rides with Duffy and declined to go with us unless I absolutely needed his help. He'd always say, "Are you kidding me? Duffy? Calm? All that screaming is *not* my idea of fun!"

I took Duffy to the pet store often. Duffy loved to pilfer cookies when we walked by the cookie bar. He was nearly 60 pounds now so he'd heave his front paws on the cookie counter and grab a mouthful of treats before I could pull him away. The clerks didn't mind. I'm glad they didn't as I had no way of calculating his loot since he'd already eaten them.

I'm brave in the car now. Mama let me ride to "Petco where the pets go." We didn't buy any pets, but I got free cookies! All kinds! Mama explained it's not a buffet. I know. It's a Table! What's a Buffet? She told Daddy I stole from it. Not me! They had lots of cookies lying around. Nobody said, "No!" Mama didn't choke me until I ate six or seven. They were all different. I tried to find my favorite, but they all tasted good.

Mama said "sorry" to the Pet Store lady. "Duffy inhaled so many I don't know how many he ate." The lady said, "It's okay. They all take one or two." If you had couth, I guess six or seven was too many. It's hard to remember that. I dropped a few on the floor for the short puppies. I thought that was nice.

Sometimes Mama took me to "Petco where the pets go" to sit on a table. She called it Scale. She said she wanted my weight. I can wait anyplace, but she liked it here best. I didn't have to go to the Vet for that. Good thing! They shot me there. Mama's happy when I'm sixty pounds. When I was a puppy, I was 250 pounds at the Vet, but that was when Daddy carried me. We got big numbers there! I liked that.

🐾 TIPS:

Start early! Take your puppy on fun rides in the car, not just trips to the vet. Get a harness or crate for the car. It'll be much safer for your dog and less stressful for you.

Pet store visits are a great place to go with your dog. There's no doubt he'll be welcome there.

The Drive-Thru

I decided to take Duffy on a short ride to get a fast food lunch. Bernard was at work so I took a chance and brought Duffy with me. He still stressed in the car but managed to calm himself enough to ride for five minutes. That is, if we didn't go to the vet. I didn't realize a disembodied voice coming from a drive-thru speaker would bring on another screaming frenzy. After ransoming our lunch from a very flustered cashier, we drove home with a bucket of hot food and a dog drooling all over the car seat.

When I recovered from the ride, I called Bernard's mother, who was in the final stages of her illness, to tell her about it. She was very weak, but she laughed uncontrollably at the whole scene, even though Bernard failed to see the humor in it.

Mama said we were going to find some lunch. I didn't know Lunch was lost, but I would help her hunt. We rode to a chicken place. She called it KFC. The place smelled good. I could smell it from far away. Far. When Mama stopped, I waited to get out. The Box by Mama's door yelled at us. I screamed loud! All of us screamed. Mama barked at me. "Stop!" I tried to stop but whined instead. My head hurt. Heart hurt. Tongue leaking all over the place. I tried to be quiet even when nobody else was quiet. Except Car Pet.

When she stopped barking at The Box, we got a big round bowl of food. Smelled like chicken. I was afraid to sniff. The Box might scream again. My tongue leaked all the way home. I got to eat some chicken later. It was good because the bowl didn't scream.

🐾 **TIPS:**

Get your puppy used to loud or sudden sounds. He will be less likely to react to them when he's older.

Don't assume that everyday sounds you recognize on your car trips will be tolerable to your dog. Think ahead and plan accordingly.

New Car

Bernard and I purchased a new car when Duffy was seven. We got a compact SUV so we could haul Duffy around in the back, away from our beleaguered ears. He still sat in the passenger seat if he and I traveled together, but now he wore his harness all the time. Bernard chose not to join us on our joyrides. He still didn't believe me when I told him Duffy behaved himself on the fun trips. Of course, that's not completely true. He still shrieked when he stressed, but the harness kept him from flinging himself around the car at stoplights like before.

Mama got me a new car. Somebody ate Trouble. Good. Maybe Mama didn't like it grumbling anymore. Our new car comes with a Car Pet too. Big one. Daddy called it SUV. Mama called it Purple Rav. I liked it. Even if it didn't smell too good. I'm working on it.

I got to ride SUV a lot. Daddy said, "Don't let Duffy hang his head out. Keep the window up most of the way so nothing flies in his eyes. Make sure his harness is tight." He had lots of rules. Mama said, "Daddy doesn't want you to get hurt. Don't worry, we'll keep you safe."

So my face is stuck In Case. My parents didn't want me to fall out. Only my nose and toes can hang out. I guess we can get extras if that happens. I won't drop them, though. They work good so far.

Mama took me on rides a couple times a week. We went around the neighborhood until SUV got trained. It's "walk, sit, and stay" worked real good. I guess it liked obedience school. Not like me. SUV went where Mama wanted. Better than Trouble. SUV didn't grumble like Trouble. I didn't scream so much anymore. Not going to the Vet. If Daddy drove, Mama sat in back. That's when we went to the Vet. I screamed and cried like before. I know these things. I've been around the block a few times. Scary.

❧ TIPS:

The way you introduce something new to your dog can make a big difference in how he accepts it.

Fun rides should involve your entire family. If not, your dog is smart enough to know when he's up for an unpleasant ride just by the people who accompany him.

Chapter 13

Katie

My Best Friend

Duffy's bleak social life with other dogs changed by a chance meeting with another Australian Shepherd named Katie. Katie was a beautiful blue merle. Her owner, Dan, had hip replacement surgery and recently started walking with a cane. He stopped to rest on a bench under a tree in the park when Duffy suddenly pulled the leash out of Bernard's hand and rushed toward Katie. Bernard yelled frantically at Duffy to stop, running as fast as he could to avert a full-on dog fight. Thankfully, Katie took a good nip at Duffy and he stopped in his tracks.

"Whew! Danger averted," Bernard sighed. He was relieved to see the standoff when he caught up with Duffy.

After apologizing to Dan for the scare, Bernard enjoyed meeting Katie and learning of Dan's recovery. Katie and Duffy got along well after the first nip. Duffy ran and played with his new friend. She was as agile as Duffy and put his domineering ways to rest.

Before leaving, Bernard told him, "I'm so glad we met you. Duffy doesn't have any dog friends. None of the dog owners accept him because they think he's aggressive. He won't hurt other dogs. He just wants to get their attention." Bernard hoped Dan would bring Katie to the park regularly to play with Duffy.

I met Dan and Katie on one of the few walks I made to the park with Bernard and Duffy. I was amazed that Duffy had a friend who tolerated him. He was happy and content in her company. He never had another friend like Katie.

I have a new friend, Katie. Daddy and I met Katie one day at the park. Her daddy met my daddy when I was on my dog-on-a-mission. Daddy says that's how I walk when I'm hunting for good mail. I have to guard my estate every day. Mama said that's my job. We found Katie on my estate, but it was okay. She looked like my mom at first.

I ran fast before Daddy could choke me. I ran up and jumped on her. She got mad and bit me. Just like my mom. I don't think girls like me jumping on them. Ginger didn't. My daddy got mad too, but her daddy laughed and let Katie play with me.

Katie's daddy said she was a rescue. I guess that means she rescued him. She was abandoned. A bandage? Confused. She looked good now. No bandages.

She lost her first rescue, but she did okay. Her daddy loved her because she saved him. Now, she has a nice home like me, even though she didn't get kidnapped.

Katie's daddy had a stick like Broom Monster, but no grass hat. It's not so scary. He didn't chase us with it. He just leaned on it. I guess he wished he had four paws like us. We ran fast!

Katie's pretty. Wink, wink. Her eyes were mixed up. One was blue and the other was brown like mine. Daddy said she's an Aussie too. I haven't seen Aussie One so I couldn't compare. Her daddy said she's a blue merle, but she doesn't look sad. No poopie butt either. Our daddies are so confused.

I'm three. Katie's older than me. She's five. She's been around the block a few times. She smelled real nice. I sniffed her a lot. She sniffed me too. I smelled her ear and it whacked me back. Not hard. She just shook her head. Her butt smelled like she ate good, but no cat food. I'll have to bring her some one day.

She runs fast like me. I liked that. I could catch her, but sometimes she flew back and I'd roll myself. I got dizzy, but I could take it. Daddy let me run without my dress. Katie too. We ran round and round a long time. Long. At least ten minutes. My tongue was leaking and I had to lie down. Katie too. We rolled in the grass together until Daddy got us water. I liked Katie a lot. She's not stinky like Jingles.

I didn't get to see Katie every day. Too bad. We looked for her all the time. Daddy's sad when she's not at the park. Me too. Then we go dog-on-a-mission. Just reading mail was boring. Sometimes Mama would come to help Daddy and me look for Katie. When we found her, we were all happy.

Katie's daddy is old. Old. At least ten. He had one paw like my tree. I tried to chew it, but everybody yelled at me. "No!" Katie got mad too. I stayed far when she was mad. Not good to make a girl mad. She bit hard like my mom. Her daddy laughed, but I still stayed far.

Daddy said, "Chicken!" I looked, but I didn't see any.

One day, we went to the park to bury bones. Katie was waiting in our favorite play spot where I didn't have to wear my dress. She could smell real good! She was sniffing before we got there. Daddy said he had one bone for her and one for me. We played and chewed our bones. I drank some water. Hey! She stole my bone! I barked and chased her. She was happy. I barked more. My bone! She ran fast! I caught up, but she turned away again. This was hard work! I wanted my bone! Nobody steals my bone. Not even Jingles. Not fair! Katie's happy. Our daddies too. I ran back and saw Katie's bone. Hah! Now I stole her bone. She dropped mine and chased me. Yippee! I'm happy now! We ran for a long time. Long. At least ten minutes. Then we rolled and barked and let our tongues leak. That was a good day!

 TIPS:

Your dog will recognize another of his own breed quite readily. They may be the best companions for your dog because their instincts and behaviors are so similar.

Observe your dog's behavior with his kin. Their interactions can teach you a lot about their breed.

We saw Lee one day when I was playing with Katie. Rusty and Dusty, the sausage terriers, came to play too, but they're too fat to run. Katie bowed a few times, but Rusty just sat down. Dusty went back to Lee for cookies. Katie liked me better anyway.

Lee made us sit and wait for cookies. She said we were really cute. Katie got a lot of cookies because she's new. She sat on my paw so I couldn't reach my cookie. Girls are like that. Sneaky.

Sometimes we saw my other friends, but they stayed far. Their parents didn't want me to run over their puppies. They liked Katie, but said I didn't have any manners. Daddy kept me away. I have lots of manners. Mama said I had couth. I think that's manners. At least I don't say "grrrr" and bark bad things like their puppies. I'm a good boy.

McKenzie came to the park one day. Everybody left. Even Katie. I tried to play with McKenzie, but she wouldn't let me bark in her ear. She ran too fast. I couldn't catch up. I tried. I ran until my tongue was leaking all over. I had to hang it to the side to breathe. Daddy said, "That's a Greyhound for you." I don't get it. She still looks brown to me.

Sassy is a small puppy they called a Sheltie. I think that meant she didn't get out much, just like Fred. Her mama said Katie was a good girl, but I needed work. Don't know Work, but I tried.

She told Daddy that she could show him how to walk me. I walked fine! She showed Daddy how to pull on my dress. We did a lot of flybys and flybacks. Mostly flybys. She was a lot of fun! She was slow, but I made her fast. She screamed and barked the whole time. She didn't do flybacks too good either. She tried to make me stop but didn't pull as hard as Daddy, so we ran a lot. All around the park! We had a good time! I liked Work. A lot!

She had to leave with Sassy real quick though. She threw my dress at Daddy when she left. Good. I didn't want to live like a Sheltie and not get out much. She never Worked me again. Too bad. I had fun! Our daddies laughed a lot that day. Daddy even laughed all the way home.

🐾 TIPS:

People mean well when they try to show you how to train your dog. Sometimes their tips may be helpful, sometimes not. In the end, you are the one who knows your dog best.

Use a trained professional to help you solve behavior problems.

Katie's Story

Duffy had four great years with Katie before we decided to move to a new neighborhood. Duffy was seven by then and Katie nearly ten. We told Dan about our plans and he wished us good luck on our move. We had a few months to wait for the house to be completed, but the move meant Duffy wouldn't see Katie again. Katie was so good for Duffy. She was truly a blessing!

As we discussed our move, Katie became very agitated. Duffy sensed her distress. It's as though she knew play time with her friend would soon be over. Her behavior affected us all. We realized how much Dan meant to us too.

One day, I told Katie my parents said we're moving. I don't get it. I thought we moved all the time. Katie was sad. No, Katie was more than sad. Worried. A lot. Her eyes got big. She walked around a lot. Fast. She's been around the block a few times. She said her first mama and daddy told her that too, and she never saw them again. They came back too late. All alone. By herself in the house. She said they went far away. Far. At least ten blocks. Gone a long time. Long. Katie had to potty in the house because they were gone real long. She didn't eat for a long time. They must be lost. The Neighbor heard her crying. Somebody came. She didn't know who. She was scared. They put a dress on her and took her away. She tried to stay. Her mama and daddy would worry. Had to stay! She fought hard, but she was too weak. They kidnapped her before her mama and daddy came home. She was sad because their hearts would hurt and she couldn't make it better.

She said Somebody took her to a big house with lots of dogs. Cats too. She was afraid they might hurt her. A Vet was in the house. The Vet poked her with a lot of Bumble Bees. They put her in a small room with a gate. She tried to get out. It cut her paws. Bleeding. Hurt a lot. Tried to lick, but they wrapped her with bandages. I knew bandages! Not good!

It was noisy. Lots of barking and whining. She heard the dogs but couldn't see them. Everybody was scared. The smell was everywhere. Worse than her Vet. It made her more scared. She didn't want them to kill her. Nobody was safe. Her mama and daddy would never find her. Poor Mama and Daddy. She cried for them because they were lost.

Lots of humans came to play with her and feed her, but Katie's mama and daddy never came. They must be so worried. Nobody to tell them where she went. One day a new Somebody came to give her a bath. The lady was nice, but not her mama. Even the smelly stuff was not like her mama. She was sad. Whined a lot. The lady gave her a kiss, but still not like her mama.

After her bath, she lived in another room with a gate. She didn't go back to the old one, but this was still the same. Cold floor. Hard walls. She heard dogs barking and whining, but couldn't see. She tried to talk to them, but nobody listened. They smelled better but still the same. Lots of humans came by to see her. Nobody took her home to look for Mama and Daddy.

One day, her new daddy came. She didn't know this was her new daddy yet. He sat in a chair that walked, but had a stick with him. She was afraid. Her old daddy hit her with a stick before. Hurt. Afraid. The Vet put her dress on and took her out to see him. She was shaking, but he was nice. She liked how he rubbed her head and neck. He called her "Katie." How did he know her name? Smart.

He said, "You want to go home with me?"

Katie thought he was going to take her home to her mama and daddy. She was happy! She licked him a lot. She tried to sit in his chair. No space. He laughed. He was happy too. "I guess you do!" He laughed. He gave her a big hug and she went with him to his home.

She waited a long time for him to take her home. Long. Three days. Katie was sad. He broke his promise. Still, he fed her good food and played with her even though he couldn't get out of his chair. He loved her. She could tell. He needed her a lot so she decided to stay until her mama and daddy came.

One day, he lost his chair that walked. Somebody stole it. He wasn't mad. He walked good with his stick now. Every time they went out, he walked better. "Katie," he said, "look how much you helped me!"

He said it was time to go to the park. Katie was so happy! Mama and Daddy used to go to the park! Maybe she was going home! Katie wanted to run there, but new daddy hurt. Katie walked slow so he could keep up.

First time at the park, no Mama and Daddy. Sad. Sniffed around a lot looking for them. New daddy tried to keep up, but had to sit down. Pain. She sat too. Maybe Mama and Daddy were lost forever. That's okay. New daddy needed me now.

She saw a big black dog running to her. That's when she met me. She was scared at first. She barked loud. "Stay away!" He might hurt new daddy.

New daddy scared too. Katie got mad when I jumped on her. She bit me. My face remembered. My mom did that when I was little. She said, "Good." I thought it was bad but didn't say so. Not safe. Girls bite. Even if her name isn't Ginger.

Some days she still thinks about her mama and daddy, but new daddy was so much nicer. She got to read new mail every day and he didn't hit her like her old daddy. Katie said new daddy had a hip place so he needed his cane. Walking chair is gone now. He told my daddy that Katie made him get better every day. She liked that. He gives her lots of good food and treats and toys. Now, she had her own friend. I think she meant me.

 TIPS:

Shelter and rescue dogs make fine pets. They sometimes come with physical or emotional baggage, but lots of love and care will make these dogs your own in no time.

Don't lose your cool or hit your dog when you're angry. He will figure out what you want soon enough. Patience is key.

Learn everything you can about your dog before you adopt. Be sure you are able to give him the care and love he needs so he'll have a "forever" home.

Your dog lives in the moment. He'll teach you how too.

Chapter 14

Moving

A New House

We chose a lot for a new house shortly after Duffy turned seven. We bought our dream home. Bernard and I waited four months in eager anticipation for our move. During that time, we culled through our belongings to see what was worth keeping and what could be thrown out or given away. We lived in our home for fourteen years and accumulated many things that we'd forgotten about or hadn't use for years. We finally found an opportunity to discard our unwanted junk. Many items were new enough to be worthwhile additions to another person's home so we delivered several truckloads to the Salvation Army receptacles.

Duffy enjoyed rummaging through the closets, drawers, and cabinets with us. He inspected all the items before we put them in boxes. Then he inspected the boxes before Bernard packed them into his truck.

At the same time, we started buying the smaller items we needed to furnish our new home. Again, Duffy inspected each bag we brought into the house before we boxed them away. He enjoyed snooping through the bags and boxes until we started packing his toys away the night before our move. That's when Duffy's stress level started to rise.

Soon, the Salvation Army's pickup truck and the movers arrived for our furniture. When they left, Bernard and I loaded my SUV with boxes for the first of four trips to our new house. Bernard did the heavy work of transferring the boxes while I stayed at the new house to unpack and wait for deliveries to arrive. We thought we had a great system planned, but didn't realize how much our activities affected Duffy and Jingles.

We're moving! My parents are really excited. I move all the time and don't get excited. Something is different. Lots of yipping in the house. Even Daddy is excited. Not like Daddy. He only gets excited when he barks and growls at me. I told my stupid sister, but she doesn't know what I said. Stupid. Sad. Nobody smart to talk to.

I guess Mama and Daddy wanted to find new mail. Nobody told us anything we didn't know before. Mama said we lived here fourteen years. I don't think she can count. I'm only seven.

Mama bought new toys for the house. I tried to see. She let me sniff, and then hid it in a box. No treats or toys for me. Boring.

My parents put our stuff in boxes so humans could steal them. This stuff didn't have paws, so they didn't go far. I think the ones with paws got stolen fast. Daddy put boxes in the back of his truck and drove away. When he came back, the boxes were gone. Maybe they're like my sister that got stolen first. All the truck boxes got new homes.

A lot of the boxes stayed for a long time. If they put me in one, I would fight to get out. No food. Or cookies. Or toys to play with.

Mama said we had four months to wait. That's a long time. Long. It must be at least a week. I know a week. It's when Mama's home, and then she's not. Daddy said Mama goes to work. I guess she hunts for food. Sometimes she comes back with cookies. Yum! I would go hunting with her, but I still remember the talking box she called KFC. Heart attack! Uh-uh. Not going there again!

Mama said the big day was here. Almost all the boxes were gone. Now she put my stuff in a box. Hey! All my toys were in the box. Mama kidnapped them! Just like she kidnapped me. My stuff! Mine! Mama and Daddy left a couple times before, but I'm worried now. My toys! Mine! I have to guard my box. Now I know how my mom felt when I got kidnapped!

Later, two old guys took my bed and sofa. Popo's bed too. Then my no-coffee table. They even took Daddy's "hell to pay" chair. Still stinky, but nobody noticed. They took my begging table where I ate with a fork. And my toys! Daddy said "leave it" when I tried to guard it. I whined, but he didn't hear. Why did he want to leave it, and then take it away? I needed to panic! Everybody's leaving but me! Rooo! All I had was my stupid sister. Rooo! She doesn't know. Maybe it's better to be stupid. I remembered Katie's story. I needed to panic again!

I cried for a long time. Long. Over ten minutes. Lots more than ten minutes. My heart hurt. It ran all over and my tongue leaked. I'm an orphan. Mama told me about orphans. She said that's when you lose your mama and daddy, like her. I didn't lose them. They lost me. Rooo!

I gave up crying. No food. Or cookies. Breakfast was a long time ago. Long. All day. I drank some water. I talked to Jingles. Daddy's right. Nobody's home there. Like talking to myself. And hearing it come back. Daddy said that's an echo. Jingles echoed all the time. I took a nap so my heart wouldn't hurt so much.

I woke up. Somebody's coming home! It was Daddy! Yike! Yike! I screamed and cried. I'm not an orphan anymore. I was so happy I had to go pee. Out in the yard. Had to be quick so I didn't lose him again.

The last time I saw my house was late. After dinner time. Daddy tied me up in my Harness. He said I had to be quiet. I tried. Squeaking now. Whining not allowed. It was hard, but I didn't want to lose him. Just In Case. I hoped he didn't lose Mama. Some boxes that didn't get stolen came with us. Daddy must've told them noise was not allowed. Or they might get lost. They made quiet noises but didn't move. Me too.

We rode a long time. Long. At least twenty minutes. We got to a new house. Not the Vet's. Daddy said, "We're home!" I don't get it. I thought we just left home. He got confused a lot.

Daddy untied me. I went inside. Everything smelled funny. I smelled lots of humans, but nobody's here. Maybe they got stolen. I found my toys. They were hiding in a box, but I knew they were there. I poked and scratched with my paws until Daddy opened it. Free at last! Not scared anymore. I checked to make sure everybody came together. Mama was there, too. Yippee! Rooo! Not lost! Mama said I made a mess, but she wasn't mad. She laughed and hugged me and I hugged back. I wanted my Girlfriend. And duck. And spider. And dinner.

Mama had the same idea. My dinner was just like at our lost house. I was hungry from panic. I didn't like panic. My head hurt. And my heart. I almost had a heart attack from panic. Like at KFC. My tongue leaked a lot. The house got all wet.

Daddy went to pick up Jingles and her gourmet food. Mama gave me some fast food. It was pretty slow to me, but I ate some anyway. My stupid sister came home by then. She screamed a lot and ran around looking for a chance to escape. I guess she couldn't find any rats. I'm glad. I ate good. Didn't want rats for dinner.

I looked for my sofa and bed. They were missing. Only the no-coffee table and begging table were there. Where was my bed? I only found stinky new house grass to sleep on. I missed my bed. I even missed Daddy's "hell to pay" chair. We lost them. The two old men too. I hoped they weren't crying somewhere in a box. Sad.

Mama and Daddy wanted me to jump real high. They told me to go Upstairs. I never saw Upstairs before. I tried to jump to the top but missed. A couple times. Tripped on my paws. Hurt, but I'm brave. My tongue was leaking. Because it was hard. Mama showed me how. I learned real quick once she showed me. We went Upstairs and then Downstairs. It all looked the same to me, but they called it something different every time. Daddy was Upstairs. Mama was Downstairs. Like learning the doggie door. Now, instead of in and out, it's up and down. I ran up. I ran down. A kazillion times. At least six. I worked hard and learned something new. I guess that's why we had to move. Nothing new there. It's all new here. Cookies too.

When I finally was smart enough for Up and Down, Daddy showed me my new bed. Rooo! Big bed. High. Soft. Rooo! I loved my bed even though it smelled funny. Have to work on it to make it smell better. I rolled a lot. All over the bed. Mama and Daddy laughed. I made them happy. There's wind up in the sky. Mama called it a Fan. Daddy made it blow. Without touching it. How did he do that? I turned upside down and let my tongue hang out. Cool. I love my bed. And my Fan.

I looked for the doggie door, but it's missing. It's lost too. Daddy said no doggie door for me. I had to keep my potty to myself until somebody figured out I had to pee or poop. I know how so I'm okay. We looked for the yard and it's lost too. We lost a lot of things on the way. The new yard was brown. Only dirt. Embarrassing. No grass to eat. There's a fence but nobody to see. Everything is brown. Even the gate. Boring. I looked for a good place to go, but it's all boring. Nothing to read while I poop.

We went back to my bed and I thought about all the mail I'll get to read soon. I had a new estate to check out. Can't wait. Can't think anymore. My eyes were rolling down and my head was hanging low. I worked hard today. Panic was hard work. So was heart attack. It's time to sleep.

We had two more old guys come visit the next day. I got to bark. A lot. Daddy threw me out in the brown yard to talk to myself. Undignified. I needed to see who. They brought stuff. I needed to see! I ran and barked in my brown yard. They left before I could smell them. Too late. I had to smell the stuff they brought. They left a sofa and two of Daddy's chairs. One is Mama's and the other is a new "hell to pay." I couldn't tell which yet, but Daddy will let me know.

My sofa was tied up. Daddy took the bandages off and I jumped on it to see if it was like my bed. Mama said, "Off!" Daddy said, "Duffy's part of the family. What's ours is his." Alpha daddy. Good boy. So I got my sofa. It's not as good as my bed, but better than my old sofa. It needed work so I rolled as much as I could. We had a Fan in here too. I could lie upside down with my tongue out Upstairs or Downstairs. I'm a happy boy.

Jingles at Our New Home

Duffy was a willing passenger riding to our new home. He'd had enough of the empty old house. It didn't work that way for Jingles. Bernard couldn't find her and searched for an hour before she returned home. He packed her and the final boxes in the car as she yowled in panic. After he returned, he discovered Jingles had peed all over the back seat. My new car! It wasn't even six months old! Bernard hoped Nature's Miracle would clean up the smell. I was furious and Bernard now had second thoughts about bringing her with us.

When we moved, they brought my stupid sister too. I didn't know why. Jingles did a big "No, no. Bad!" last night when nobody was looking. She peed in Mama's new car. Daddy took to the bottle again with "thank heaven for Nature's Miracle." Good thing he found it. Mama was mad. Real mad. Mad. We locked my stupid sister in the house even though Mama was ready to leave her to the wildlife. We stayed far. No Broom Monster in sight, but Mama had ways to give you what for. Not like the Gingers or my mom, but just as bad. Scary.

Mama and Daddy said Jingles had to stay inside all the time now because there's more wildlife nearby. I'm glad. I'm pretty wild so we can have lots more fun. Jingles didn't like it, though. She made lots of noise at night. Daddy got real mad when she did.

Daddy gave her a new secret room. I could sneak in for gourmet food sometimes, but Daddy would growl and chase me out. It's fun!

Once I almost got to Jingles' little box, but Daddy was fast this time. No luck.

Our New Neighbors

We were one of nine new families moving in on our cul-de-sac. We met our neighbors quickly and happily showed off our new homes to each other. Duffy made a positive impression on everyone. He enjoyed the attention.

Our new house is nice, but we have new neighbors too. My parents ran around in everybody's house. I guess they were looking for our stolen boxes. All gone, but they're happy anyway. The neighbors must have them so they weren't far away.

I'm the king here. Nobody had dogs. Or cats. Just us. Mama and Daddy said Jingles had to stay inside because we had Coyotes. I didn't know where they lived or what they looked like. Maybe they're in the stolen boxes. Daddy said they could eat Jingles. Eeek! She's stupid but still my sister. I didn't want them to eat her! Especially if they left her stuffing behind. Eww!

🐾 **TIPS:**

Moving can be an ordeal for your dog as well as for humans. Plan his move as carefully as you would for your family, furniture, and possessions.

Once the move is over, be as consistent with his old routine as possible. This will help your dog adjust to his new environment.

Reassure your pet if he is having a rough adjustment. This is when he needs your attention most.

Chapter 15

Breaking the Sound Barrier

Lawnmowers and Vacuum Cleaners

Duffy's herding instincts drove him to circle and bark at the lawn mower and vacuum cleaner when they were in use.

He loved to get his face right up to the exhaust when Bernard started the lawn mower. Then he'd run ahead of it to block it from moving forward. Duffy's barking and lunging worried Bernard. He was afraid that one day Duffy's paws might get caught under the mower blades. Often he'd have to wield the broom as the quickest deterrent for Duffy's frantic behavior.

In the house, Duffy herded the vacuum cleaner. Chores took twice as long to complete when Duffy was on guard.

Daddy has some bad toys. Not like mine. One has gas. Daddy's yard toy is big. Big. He called it Lawn Mower. It was stinky and noisy. I tried to give it what for, but Daddy always chased me away. He said I'm a nuisance. I always got new scents because of the gas. I had to sniff to see if I missed something. Like cookies! Yum! My favorite!

The lawn mower was real loud and ate lots of grass. Every time Daddy chased it around the yard it made stinky gas. I don't eat grass too much anymore. I didn't want gas. Gas could sneak up and poke me in my rootie-toot when I'm not looking. I always checked to see if anything's missing. I'm okay. Just reminded me of dinner. Woke me up sometimes. Gas dreams could be hell to pay. Couldn't catch them. They barked and ran. Too fast for me to see.

Daddy had a house toy too. He called it Vacuum Cleaner. I don't know why it's Cleaner. It didn't look any cleaner from last time. It just ran in the same place over and over. Just like my flybys and flybacks. It went one way, Daddy pulled it back. Daddy didn't take it to obedience school. It wore a dress too but didn't go for walks like me. Daddy watched it a lot so it wouldn't get lost. Nobody takes Vacuum Cleaner out. Must be a Sheltie. It couldn't go anywhere by itself. Not smart like me. It whined a lot but had nothing to say. Sad.

I always had to be around to help when Daddy played with his toys. I brought my toys too, so they could see what to do. Daddy got mad and barked real loud. Then he'd throw my toys at me. Whee! Playtime! Sometimes he got Broom Monster to help. Scary. I stayed far then. My toys never learned anything. That's why they laid around all the time with nothing to do.

Fourth of July

We moved to our new house a few days before the Fourth of July. It was an exciting time for us. That evening, we saw five fireworks displays from our bedroom window. We realized we had the best view on our hill. Duffy didn't like the noise, but he managed to find a dark, quiet spot to hide while Jingles ran to her safe haven to yowl the night away.

Lots of excitement at our new house. I didn't know why there's so much noise outside, but I got scared just the same. Lots of booms, but not on TV like at our old house. My parents sat on the bed and looked out the window. When the booms started, I went to a dark hidey-hole Daddy called Closet. I didn't like booms. I'm not crying, but can't stop my tongue from leaking. Hot! I had to breathe hard. My face was shaking. Mama came to hug me. My rootie-toot is hugging my butt door. Jingles didn't come with me. She went to find her little box and cried from there. I couldn't fit or I would go there too.

The booms left fast, so we got to sleep on time. I kept listening to make sure, but they left. I put my rootie-toot near Mama. Just in case.

Hot Air Balloons

We were surprised one day by a hot air balloon flying above our new house. More soared by every afternoon. We were on their daily summer flight path. We enjoyed the colorful balloons and looked forward to waving to the people in the baskets.

The hot air balloons intimidated Duffy. He made it a point to run indoors whenever they flew overhead. The immense shape and low whoosh from the balloons frightened Duffy badly the first time it appeared. He shrieked and flew to his safe spot in the house. He needed a great deal of comforting until the balloon sailed out of sight.

I think I found some wildlife. Not fun! We saw big balls that growled in the sky. They ate humans. I saw body parts hanging out. First time I saw one I yiked! Eeek! Eeek! I screamed and ran to my hidey-hole. Mama came too. I tried to be brave so she wouldn't be scared. My heart ran fast. She just hugged me until my tongue stopped leaking. Mama's braver than me!

I found out they came all the time. Sometimes over our house, looking for more humans to eat. Daddy's brave. Mama too. They just watched and waved. The ball didn't know Downstairs so we were safe. Good. Jingles disappeared. Finally smart.

Blue Angels

The Blue Angels flew in our neighborhood once a year. The precision flying impressed us. Bernard was raised in the military so he looked forward to their yearly return. We went to see them perform at the nearby base years before we moved, but now they flew right over our home. We enjoyed watching them and taking photos of their routines. Occasionally, they'd sneak up and startle us as their jet engines roared by. Duffy bolted into the house on those occasions. He tried to be brave, but there were limits to his courage.

Now we have more wildlife! Big Bird. Big. Bigger than the crows. Daddy showed me eagles but they're way bigger. He calls them Blue Angels. More noise. I told them not allowed, but they're noisy anyway. Bad Birds. Daddy's happy. He put big cups on his eyes. To see better. Daddy said they're binoculars, but they looked like cups to me. I don't get it. I saw good without cups on my eyes.

He said the Blue Angels only come once a year. Good. I hope that's longer than a week. They snuck around and then screamed when you didn't look. Daddy laughed when I freaked out. Not fair! I ran to my hidey-hole until they're gone. Just in case they had the blues all over the yard. Or poked on my head like the blue jays. Must be related.

They showed up again and again. I still got scared but not so much anymore. They didn't come downstairs. I just didn't like it when they snuck up and screamed when I wasn't looking. Not funny.

🐾 **TIPS:**

Your dog may react to loud or sudden sounds. Vacuum cleaners, lawn mowers, and coffee grinders are common offenders, but some sounds are unforeseen. Get him accustomed to all kinds of sounds at an early age.

Don't overreact when he gets scared, but don't coddle him either. Relax and comfort him until he gets over his fright. Talk gently to help him understand that there's no reason for worry.

If he's unable to cope when certain fearful situations occur, get a sedative from your vet to calm him.

Chapter 16

Homeland Security

Sled Dog

Duffy's walks were a daily challenge. He pulled like a sled dog, so I couldn't take him on walks alone. He had two agendas. At the start of each walk, Duffy gleefully dashed from spot to spot inspecting his mail. Though he didn't mark his territory, Duffy searched for anything new in the neighborhood. His confrontations told every trespassing dog to stay off his estate.

In order to burn as much of Duffy's energy as possible, Bernard often walked him five or more miles from home. Even then, Bernard had to be mindful of sudden changes of direction or demeanor in Duffy's behavior. Walks became stressful and often aggravating. A few times, they were downright dangerous.

Daddy and I went for long walks every day. Even when it's hot. He needed the exercise. We went when no dogs were around. Daddy said Lunchtime. I liked lunch, but nobody gave me any. The dogs knew the rules. Otherwise, I had to give them what for. It's fun when it's cold outside. Too much work when it's hot.

Most days, we went slow. Daddy couldn't keep up with me. I tried to go faster, but then I choked. Daddy kept saying, "You're not a sled dog." I saw Snow Dogs once on TV. It's a movie. They put their daddy on a sled and ran all the way to Alaska. Must be far away. At least three blocks! I wanted to go to Alaska where it's cold, but I didn't have a sled. Daddy needed slide shoes if we went. His shoes had brakes so I couldn't run too fast.

Once I pulled my daddy too fast. Daddy was mad at me because he fell down. In the road. He told Mama he slipped on gravel. I ran on it, but didn't see Gravel. What's Gravel? I stayed close when he fell. Cars were barking. Humans barking too. Everybody mad but me. I had to rescue him so he doesn't bring Broom Monster next time to lean on. Scary!

Standoff

Duffy managed to create unpleasant incidents quite often on his walks. Bernard changed his route often to avoid meeting other dogs, but it wasn't always possible.

Daddy and I walked every day all over our estate. That's what Mama called outside. It's big so we walked different places every day.

We saw a new dog walking around. He was big, but I wasn't scared. I barked to tell him he was on my estate. He didn't like my bark so he growled back at me. I was mad because he tried to bite me. Daddy pulled me away. I fought hard. This is my estate. Mama said. This time, I couldn't do my flyby. Daddy pulled hard. I was choking, but nobody's supposed to be tougher than me on my estate. Daddy pulled harder. My neck got real skinny. I heard a lot of banging in my ears. The big dog and his human ran down the street. My choke chain broke. I tried to chase him, but Daddy screamed at me. I thought he got hurt so I came back. I had to bring him home for water. Me too. My neck was itchy, but I was still mad.

Mama Gets Hurt

Against my better judgment, I took Duffy for a walk on my own one day. Duffy surprised me by being cooperative and calm. I wondered if I had the right dog!

We neared the park where a group of firemen ran laps and exercised. As I walked through the park, I stepped on an uneven patch of grass and turned my ankle. I fell to the ground hard as Duffy stood by protecting me. My ankle hurt badly so I stayed on the ground for several minutes as the firemen ran past us. No one helped me, even the fireman sitting in the truck who witnessed my fall. I couldn't understand their disinterest. Duffy, my great protector, gave me lots of kisses and guarded me until I managed to pull myself up. He walked carefully by my side all the way home. When I told Bernard what happened, he asked, "Are you sure you walked *Duffy*?"

Mama took me out on a walk one day. She didn't go much because Daddy said I'm a dog-on-a-mission and nobody could walk me. Especially Mama. But I try. Slow, but I try.

We walked to the park and Mama sat on the grass. She hurt her paw. She said it was her ankle, but I know a paw when I see one. I saw my chance to give her lots of licks, but she made me sit too. It was hard because she was so close to my face. Lots of humans ran around, but they stayed far. My Mama! Mine!

When she got up, she walked funny. She was mad, but not at me. She saw humans called Firemen playing in the park, but they didn't stop to help. I didn't want Fire coming our way. That's what Daddy used for barbecue. They might cook us and Mama's real slow so we wouldn't get away. I was glad when we walked home. I was a real good boy and didn't do any flybys. I knew I had to walk slow so Mama wouldn't get lost. Her paw whined too much.

Daddy saw us when we got home. Mama said I was a good boy even though he didn't believe it.

Claiming My Territory

Duffy never lacked courage in the face of an enemy. He dared dogs to take him on, but more so if they were very large. Bernard is strong, but not as strong as Duffy. I worried that one or both might someday be seriously injured.

Daddy told Mama we saw a big dog on my estate. Big. Daddy said it was a German Shepherd. His Mama was small. Small. Maybe she's a Poodle. He didn't bark German. I knew what he said. It wasn't nice, German or not. He tried to steal my estate. We gave him what for. Daddy didn't growl, but he got tense, even though he doesn't have a lot of hair to stand up. I knew I had to do something. Daddy was counting on me. I barked and howled and pulled. A lot. Daddy didn't let me go dog-on-a-mission. He held me back until the big dog and his mama disappeared. I choked until I fell asleep. Then I woke up. I didn't see where they went, but they were gone by then. Daddy said I passed out. I didn't think I passed anything because I was still in the same spot, but I'm glad the big dog knew who was boss. His mama too.

Daddy was real wet when I got up. He told Mama he thought he'd have to break up a dog fight because the big dog's mama was 100 pounds dripping wet and couldn't hold her dog. I guess big dog's mama shook and got Daddy wet when I was sleeping. Mama found out how brave I was even though I passed out. He said, "Duffy pulled so hard his tongue was purple!" I'm glad. That's Mama's favorite color. I have to do that again when Mama can see. I never saw where the big dog and his mama went. I think I missed something when I fell asleep.

Mama said I didn't have a lick of sense. I'm still looking where to lick, but most times I just smell scents. Too confusing. Maybe someday they'll tell me what scents I can lick.

Everybody depended on me to watch my estate. My friends depended on me too. I wasn't around when Ricky saw the pit bull and got hurt. He was brave, but not a good estate guard. I had to protect my parents and my friends. Can't let just anybody come in.

They messed up all my mail, and I had to start over. Humans don't guard so good. That's why they have us. I did the best job because I'm smart.

Chasing the Coyote

After our move, we discovered our new neighborhood abutted a few acres of undeveloped land nearby for Duffy to explore. Bernard enjoyed letting Duffy run free for a few minutes each day. The builder prepared the lots for future development so most of the land lay bare with dirt and clay. Very few people had dogs here. We felt Duffy really had an estate of his own for now.

Bernard and Duffy often saw deer tracks along the trails. One day, they came upon a coyote climbing up from the canyon. The coyote turned to retreat, but Duffy followed him. Bernard chased after them, hollering loudly for Duffy to come back. He feared Duffy might disappear into the canyon and get ambushed by the pack. It was impossible to follow him down the rugged terrain.

Daddy and I walked our new estate every day. We found lots of good things to smell, but not mail. Daddy said there's deer here. Confused. Mama calls me "dear" everywhere, not just here.

Funny smells. Daddy said they're deer tracks. Not so dear. Not enough toes. Must be hurt like Ricky. Two-Toes hid all the time. We never saw him. Maybe too many bandages.

I didn't wear my dress in the field on my estate. Nobody's around. One day I thought we saw Two-Toes. I ran to see, but he ran away to hide. Daddy ran after me barking. A lot. He was excited. Real excited. Me too. Only this wasn't Two-Toes. It was a stinky dog. Living the wild life. He can't be on my estate. I was mad. I chased him down the canyon out of my estate. Good. Tell Two-Toes. Keep away.

Daddy barked loud and long. Yiking! Like me at the Vet. Daddy sounded scared, so I went back. Maybe Two-Toes was chasing Daddy. I better make sure Daddy's okay. Daddy gave me a big hug when I came. Daddy said he was scared he lost me. I knew where I was. Daddy forgot because he was scared. He made me wear my dress so he could follow me home.

Later, Daddy told Mama I chased a coyote today. Coyote tried to steal my estate. Daddy said I was lucky. "The coyote could turn on him and he'd be a goner." Never saw that. Coyote would be pretty stupid to mess with me. I'm the king. Daddy said Coyote had a pack and could attack me. Hmm. He might have food in his pack. I'll have to check next time. He must be our neighbor where Jingles went to party. Maybe he had cookies. He could smash them good when he ran home. Mmmm! I love smashed cookies. Just like Gramee used to make.

We never saw Coyote again. We saw a big brown dog once a long way off. Big. Real big. He saw us and ran away. Shy. Daddy said it was a deer. I thought he was nice too but never met him. We still never found Two-Toes. Maybe the big brown dog and Two-Toes are relatives. Both shy. They didn't come around anymore. Too much noise on our estate now.

Dog Fight on the Boulevard

As our new community grew and more people moved into the houses, it was inevitable that Duffy would run into other dogs. His aggression escalated as more dogs moved into our neighborhood. One day, Bernard and Duffy explored the far side of the field when Duffy saw another dog walking with his owner on the sidewalk, about a quarter of a mile away. Without warning, Duffy ran full speed to challenge the dog. Bernard couldn't catch up and both dogs ended up brawling on the boulevard as cars screeched and dodged the melee.

Luckily, both dogs and cars avoided damage or injury. Bernard was mortified and apologized profusely to the enraged owner who exchanged hurried words and threats before they went on their way. We hoped the other man wouldn't pursue charges for this unprovoked attack. After weeks of concerned anticipation, the incident became a distant, though unnerving memory.

Lots more dogs and humans moved here now. My estate was crowded. Too much noise from trucks and humans. Dusty. I sneezed a lot. Bad mail.

We looked for Two-Toes and Coyote in the same big field. I had to wear my dress a lot now, but not here. It's fun playing on my field. Daddy threw the ball far. Far. I ran until my paws shook. My tongue leaked a lot, but I'm happy.

A man and a dog came on my estate one day. Hey! Not on my estate! I ran to give them what for. Daddy yiked loud again. Running fast now. The big white dog turned around and barked bad things. I'm mad! We both gave each other what for. We ended up on the road. I wouldn't let go. White dog either. Both daddies yiked loud. Cars screeched. Honked. Everybody's barking. Like a big party, only everybody's mad.

Daddy pulled me back. Our daddies barked at each other. White dog moved away. Scared. Hid behind his daddy. Good. He knows I'm the king. Daddy's mad at me all the way home. He said, "Now you've done it!" I know I did. I was there. He saw it too!

Mama heard about my fight and got real scared. I licked her face. I told her I'm okay, but she's still scared. Afraid of the dogcatcher. Not worried. Nobody can catch me. Daddy said, "We're going to get sued!" I didn't know who Sue was, but I hoped she's pretty. Wink, wink.

That night, Mama treated me real nice. I got extra treats and hugs. She massaged me all over my itchy spots. White dog didn't bite hard. I rolled over and let my tongue hang out. Mama liked that because I'm cute.

Mama asked about the fight and Daddy said he didn't know who the man was. He didn't get Daddy's name either. My daddy didn't have his dress on. Lucky. Hate to see Daddy go. He can't run too fast and the dogcatcher would get him.

Klaus

Our neighbor, Dave, lived at the end of our street. He picked out a young Weimaraner for his family. Klaus was a lumbering sweet goofball whose carefree manner indicated he wanted to make new friends and play. The first time he met Duffy, Klaus received a chomp on his hindquarters. Dave chalked it up as a learning experience for Klaus, though we felt badly Duffy was so unpleasant to this meek little dog. After that experience, Klaus came to play with us, but never left his driveway whenever Duffy appeared.

We have a new dog on my estate. His name is Klaus. Mama and Daddy said it's okay to let him live here. He's not too smart. I felt sorry, so I let him stay. Daddy said he's a Weimaraner. Why ran where? I guess he ran here. Uncle Dave saved him. Not sure from where, but he's here.

One day he came to our yard to pee. I got mad and gave him what for. Right on the butt. He screamed and ran home. Daddy gave me what for right back, but not on the butt. Lots of growling and barking. Confused. This is our yard! My estate! Uncle Dave said it's okay. Klaus had to learn. That's right! I'm the king! When Daddy and I went for our walk, I told Klaus to stay away. He listened and sat on his car bed that Daddy calls driveway. Afraid. He remembered. Guess he's not that stupid.

Sometimes I let Klaus come play. He's slow. Can't catch me. No fun when we don't run fast. He stood funny when we saw birds. He wanted to chase them, but just looked instead. Nose out, one paw up. Klaus's mom didn't teach him too good. No wonder he ran here. Didn't have to work hard for food.

More Dogs in the Neighborhood

Over the years, we saw many dogs come and go in the neighborhood. The same precautions had to be made to avoid further confrontations. Bernard walked Duffy at midday when most owners weren't out. He still took Duffy on long walks. Bernard discovered a fifteen mile trail in the preserve, which they walked a number of times. Duffy was eleven by this time so returning home up a very steep incline became difficult, especially on hot days.

We walked far in the new neighborhood. No park so no new dogs to chase. Too bad. We saw some other dogs, but Daddy stayed far. I tried to fly by to sniff, but Daddy always made me fly back. I guess he wanted them to know I'm the king and I didn't make friends. Hard to be king sometimes.

🐾 TIPS:

Exercise is key when you have an energetic dog. Age may slow him down, but not as much as you'd think.

If your dog doesn't readily accept other dogs, you need to find a way to use up his energy without getting him or yourself into a dangerous situation.

Regardless of your dog's behavior with other dogs, you still need to stay aware of your surroundings when you walk. An unleashed dog could come up and surprise you. Not every dog has a responsible owner.

Be aware of wildlife in your neighborhood. A domestic dog tangling with an animal that lives in the wild might not fare well if confronted.

Chapter 17

My New Sister

My Wish Came True

After months of discussion, Bernard gave in to my appeal for another dog. I thought working with a breeder might help circumvent some of the problems we experienced with Duffy. We hoped a breeder could help us select a puppy with a more predictable temperament.

I searched the Internet for a local breeder. I found several reputable breeders within an hour's drive, but once I saw the photo of Foxie, who was the spitting image of our Duffy, on the kennel's home page, I didn't look any further. The similarity was uncanny!

I made an appointment to talk to Dayle at her kennel. She and Ron had a new litter of puppies ready for adoption in a matter of weeks, but I didn't want to make another hasty decision. I drove out to meet Dayle, and we talked at length. Dayle's forthright and informative answers gave me the confidence that we'd have a wonderful puppy. As we spoke, she asked my preference of sex and color. I thought a female with the same black-tri coloring as Duffy would be best for us.

We decided to wait for their next litter. Three months went by before Dayle called. The puppies were here. Only one black-tri female arrived in this litter so I felt this little one chose us. Bernard was enthused until he found out we wouldn't have much of a selection.

Dayle emailed a photo of our four-day-old puppy. By that weekend, we were back at their farm to look at our girl in person. She was eight days old. We brought Duffy with us so he could take a look as well. That was probably a mistake, but we wanted to be sure he'd accept another dog in our home.

Bernard was enamored by the beautiful blue merle puppies in that litter. They reminded us of Katie. There were five of them. Bernard said, "I like these puppies! They're really pretty." At that point, I was conflicted about my choice. Do we take the one I requested, or do we choose another one? Since we had first pick, I wavered. Dayle said it was up to us. Bernard noticed the black-tri girl was also the runt. That brought back memories, or rather nightmares, of our experiences with Duffy. This wasn't going to be an easy decision.

Even so, we ventured out every weekend to play with the little fur balls. Naturally, most of our attention was on our black-tri girl. During that time, we noticed she was playful but not overbearing. She wasn't headstrong or dominant either, which we liked. After a couple of weeks, we knew she was the one.

I'm getting old now. I'm twelve. At last Mama and Daddy decided to get me a sister. I have a lot of knowledge to pass on. Just in time. I hope she's smart. And pretty. Not like my own sister. Homely.

They got my new sister from a breeder. They looked like humans to me, but that's what Mama called them. Maybe because they have a paper. Which means my puppy will have a paper too. I have all kinds of papers at home, but Mama said this one was special. I guess they hid mine because I'm real special. Didn't want anyone to steal my paper. Daddy said I didn't have a paper. He's mean. Tried to hurt my feelings, but I know better. I got one from Ginger.

Mama said she chose the breeder because they had a girl who looked just like me. How can that be? Is that my stolen sister? I looked at the picture on Mama's computer, but it didn't smell like her. Didn't smell like anything. Not my stolen sister after all.

We had to wait until it was time to march. I don't know where, but Mama said the puppy was coming in March. One day, Mama was crying at the computer. She was happy. She said our puppy was born. I didn't see it anywhere, but it sounded good to me. I was ready to march out to get her, but we went in SUV instead. I don't get it. Sometimes Mama and Daddy bark funny.

I got to see my sister's family once after she was born. The breeder called the puppies Aussies too. Humans are so confused. I must be an Aussie now since nobody called me puppy anymore. I'm sure Mama wanted to kidnap this puppy because their humans were confused. They had a lot of puppies, but Mama said we would only pick one. Good. One is all I can handle. Too much to teach. Get it right the first time. She's just a puppy, though, so I have to go slow.

My sister's mother was pretty. Wink, wink. They called her Sally. Mama said Sally was a champion. She had seven puppies. You had to be a champion to have seven puppies. The puppies reminded me of my mom. The smell made me remember when I was a puppy. Long time. Long. Way long. But I still remembered. Mama said my puppy was only one week old and couldn't see me. She called my name, "Uff-uff," just like my mom did when I was little. My puppy's paws didn't work yet so she couldn't walk. She sucked on my nose when I got close. Yike! Not the mama! That's okay, though. She liked me. I could smell her and knew she was the one even though she didn't look like a puppy. Uncle Ron said, "They look like rats when they're newborn." I know rats. My puppy wasn't a rat.

We chose the cutest one. Good thing Mama and Daddy knew how to pick. I was going to show them myself, but Sally said,

"Grrrrr." She told me stay far. I'm tough, but I remembered my mom and Ginger and didn't want to take any chances. Sallys might be as bad as Gingers. Girls bite hard. Especially if you get too nosy. I looked hard to see if my puppy was the runt. That's what they called me. It must mean smart. Had to be sure. Not enough time to teach a dumb one. Nobody liked me sniffing around. Sally got mad and bit me. Sally didn't bite as hard as Ginger or my mom, but I got stuffed in SUV just the same. Just me and the Car Pet after that.

Mama and Daddy left me at home after that visit. Kept me safe from Sally. They went to see my puppy every time Mama didn't have to work. Took them a long time to kidnap her. Not like me. I guess Mama was good at it, but not Daddy.

We spent eight weekends visiting Dayle and Ron's kennel. Now, it was time to bring our girl home. The excitement of the big day overshadowed the realization that life, again, would not be the same. It finally dawned on us that our day trips to little restaurants and shops after our visits would come to an end.

Ron gave us a puppy kit with registration papers, health certificates, and other supplies and instructions. When we returned to the car, our puppy quietly whimpered as she watched her familiar surroundings disappear, but she soon settled in my lap and slept all the way home.

Duffy met us at the door. His excitement was evident, but I didn't know if he was overjoyed at having a sister or another animal to terrorize. We watched him very carefully. We introduced our pup to the yard and she entertained herself and us by walking atop the shrubs around the perimeter. She weighed hardly anything! Duffy amazed us by keeping close company, making sure she didn't get into any trouble. Our boy suddenly became a mother hen.

Our cat didn't find this pup very amusing at all. Jingles took shelter in her room when the dogs became too boisterous, but most of her waking hours were spent foraging outside away from home. She only came back to eat a little and sleep in relative safety.

I waited and waited. Long time. Long. Forever. Mama said eight weeks! One day, I knew it was time. My parents were yipping a lot. They went to get my puppy. I was right. When they got home, my puppy came to me and did her happy dance. And peed on the floor. On my paws too. Embarrassing! I knew right then she wasn't going to be tough like me. She wouldn't be alpha girl anytime soon. Too bad. Daddy said, "Thank heaven for Nature's Miracle." He took to the bottle a lot for a long time after that. Long. A month. Sad. She's not smart like me after all. Or tough. Sigh. At least she's smarter than Jingles. Not much. Must be because they're girls. At least she could talk to me. Jingles talked funny so I had to guess.

My sister looked like me, but Mama said she looked like a guinea pig. I just have to take her word for it since I don't know Guinea Pig. The breeder said the babies looked like rats at first. Not to me. I knew rats. Eww! Stinky. Cat breath! Lots of stuffing showing.

My puppy was round like my hedgehog and smelled like Frosty Paws. Yum! I licked her to check and she burped in my face. Not the same. I wondered if she had a squeaky? I decided not to bite her to find out. Daddy would give me "hell to pay" and chase me with the Broom Monster. Mama would eat me for sure.

I gave my puppy my favorite duck. She slept on it all the time. The duck was as big as her. She tried to run and shake it. The duck hit her one day and she fell down. Not her friend for a long time. At least five minutes. Just like me and my big rope toy. Not my friend either. Longer than five minutes. Long. Good thing it was my duck. Rope toy is dangerous.

My puppy liked to play a lot. She fell asleep real quick too. On my duck. One time, she fell asleep with a ball in her mouth. Daddy said she was "out like a light." I guess she should play outside to stay awake.

🐾 TIPS:

Introducing the new member of the family to your current pets is important.

When you meet a very young puppy, be sure his mother is willing to have you handle him. Mothers are very protective of their young and might not tolerate a stranger or new dog nearby.

Once your new puppy comes home, be watchful of any possible jealousies or aberrant behavior from your other pets.

Visit to the Vet

We took our pup for her first checkup. Everyone oohed and aahed at the precious little pup. She barely weighed eight pounds and still fit in my two hands. The vet gave her a booster shot and embedded a microchip in her back. She enjoyed everyone's attention at first, but learned the vet's office might not be a fun place after all.

> Mama and Daddy took my puppy to the Vet. I stayed home. Daddy said I'm a nuisance. I still didn't smell anything new, but at least I didn't have to go. Lucky me. I told her watch out for Bumble Bees. She didn't know them yet. She learned. She got the Bumble Bee. Two times. She cried. One really hurt. They got a big Bumble Bee to sting her in the back. Big. Mama said it was a chip. Except you don't eat this one.

My Sister's New Name

Finding a name for our new puppy was formidable. Besides just a household name, there was a string of other names we needed to add to her registration. This was all new to me! I looked on the Internet for ideas. I pondered a combination of her mother's and father's names, Sally and Ryder. Ryde Sally Ryde? To the Moon Sally Ryde? Does that mean I have to call her Sally or Moon? At the time, I didn't know I could call her anything I wanted. It didn't have anything to do with her registry.

I looked on the Internet again. One site described "Corrie" as the Chosen One. That she was! I liked the name. After days of searching, I came upon a website with an English-Irish dictionary. I looked up Fox and found Sionnach. So we finally had a name! Foxpointe's Sionnach Corrie! Whew! What a mouthful!

My sister finally got a name. Mama studied hard to find it. She's not too smart. She had to research. I always searched once and found what I wanted. I sniffed around, but didn't know what she was searching for.

Mama liked Echo at first. Daddy said he liked Duffy Two. I'm glad he still liked me. Mama said, "That doesn't make sense."

Daddy replied, "I don't like Echo." I didn't know Echo, but I'm glad Daddy liked me.

Mama found the name Corrie in her research. I guess that means you looked twice if you're a human. Mama said Corrie means the Chosen One. They got it right! I chose her when we all went to meet her mom. Everybody would know she's special when they heard her name.

Mama told my puppy her name is Corrie. I learned it right away, but my puppy was slow. It took a long time for her to figure out. She called me Bubby. I wasn't going to correct her. I liked my special name. Just hers for me. I called her Pup sometimes. I hoped she wasn't stupid like Jingles. That would be bad. Bad. No hope left.

Corrie was a good puppy. She didn't cry for her mom like I did when I was kidnapped. I guess her mom told her it was coming. She got to sleep in a box Mama called Crate. I remembered being stuffed in one at Gordon and Setter's house. I'm glad it was her, not me. I could see her and she could see me, but she couldn't get out. Sometimes she would cry to make me feel bad. Not letting her out, though. Didn't want her to pee on me again. No couth. She got the same Wee-Wee Pads, but a nicer space than mine when I first came home. That's okay because I have nicer house grass now. And bed. Soft.

Mama didn't train Corrie on the Wee-Wee Pad. She got up to take her outside every time Corrie moved around at night or said, "uff-uff." That's puppy talk for "let me out!" Mama would tell her to "go wee-wee." Sometimes she'd tell Corrie to "do it" and poop would come out. I guess Corrie doesn't know how to do it on her own so she followed orders. Puppies are small, but they pee and poop a lot. She would get a cookie if she did everything right. Cookies for me too. Because I kept them safe in the dark. Guarding was my job now, but sleep was better.

🐾 TIPS:

Make your first visit to the vet short and fun.

Getting a purebred dog means you have the privilege of giving him a fancy name. Whatever you name your puppy on his registry, you can call him anything you want at home.

Be consistent with potty training from the very beginning. Your dog will learn very quickly if you are. Reinforce the training with treats.

Day Care

Raising a puppy who's full of energy is taxing, frustrating, and painful. Her needle-like claws and teeth drew a lot of blood in the weeks and months that followed. Many times, Bernard and I wanted a break. We blockaded the play area and jumped over the barrier, leaving Corrie to stay with Duffy. Otherwise, we'd put her in her crate if we left the house. Duffy was our puppy sitter during those times.

Some days, Corrie would play so much that my parents would escape. Especially when Corrie would bite or scratch. Which was a lot. That's when they needed Time-Out. Then they'd leave when I'm not looking. I got a new job. Puppy slave.

Corrie had a kazillion toes and teeth. She liked to jump all over me and eat my ears and face. Puppy teeth are like Bumble Bees! Her mouth was itchy so she had to chew. Sometimes I rolled Corrie if she played too hard, but I'm tough. I could take abuse. That's what happens when you're a puppy slave. No Time-Out. I'm not the mama!

Jingles was getting very old, but she still preferred her outdoor life. Sometimes she wouldn't come home for days. She was either becoming more feral or just didn't enjoy having a young puppy around terrorizing her. When she did come home, she'd disappear into her safe haven to sleep.

My stupid sister ran and hid when she saw Corrie coming. She remembered the wall she hit when I was a puppy. No reruns for Jingles. Dangerous.

Jingles was old. Way old. At least a couple tens. She looked at me funny sometimes. She screamed and ran to her secret room or went away for days. She came home with rat breath. Daddy looked for leftovers with his yard spoon when she did. He said it's disgusting, but he still kept it in a big can to give to the neighbors.

Corrie learned a little bit every day. She had small brains so she couldn't think too long. Most days, she played and slept. She ate too. A lot! She won't be a good estate dog. She's not tough like me. All she does is pee on humans and dogs. One time, she peed on neighbor Dave's new shoes. Daddy felt bad. Not me. I liked Dave's happy dance. Lots of yips too!

Corrie ran on top of the yard plants every day. Mama said it's because she's small. Almost got stuck in the fence once, but I saved her. Sometimes small isn't a good thing. I told her about the fat bunny that got stuck in the fence on our estate. Nobody ate him, but he was dead all the same. She listened good. Her eyes got big and she sat down. Good. Sitting made her brains work. She's careful now. She didn't know bunny yet, but she made sure not to get stuck.

Mama carried Corrie a lot when she was a puppy. Mama would growl, "Incorrigible!" when she did. Must be the name they put on her paper, but we called her Corrie. When she was bad, Mama would pick her up and take her inside. Then I would be puppy slave.

Corrie asked me, "Bubby, what happened?" Too much explaining. She'll have to figure it out herself. Sometimes it's better to learn on your own. Nobody told me and I ended up a genius.

My days of lying on the sofa are gone. My stupid sister used to sleep on the top pillow. She would be chief guard, so I got a lot of beauty sleep. That's why I'm so pretty even if I'm not a girl. Jingles didn't like Corrie and wouldn't guard the sofa anymore.

It's getting warm now so I liked to lie upside down near the Fan with my face open and my paws sticking up. Only now Corrie cried when I got up on the sofa. Too much noise! So I slept on the house grass. Then she'd lie on me. Hot! I told her I'm not the mama. She wouldn't listen. My tongue leaked a lot and I didn't even have my Girlfriend. Corrie played with it now. She ate a hole in it one day. "No, no! Bad girl!" She's going to be dinner now! Mama saw the hole and growled at her, but she was safe. Mama must feel sorry for her because she's a girl. Good thing she's not fat enough yet. I reminded her of the fat bunny. She's wise now. No new holes in my green blanket. Mama thought Corrie learned pretty quick because she growled at her, but we knew the truth.

Corrie wasn't tough like me. She guarded when I guarded, but behind. She ran home if she's afraid. I told her she wasn't alpha girl. Alpha dogs worked hard. It's like being king, like me. I had to be on guard all the time. To keep the estate safe. No dogs or bad humans allowed. No friends. No long trips away from home. She's better off.

🐾 TIPS:

Keep him occupied with durable chew toys or treats. The treat should be for puppies. Some treats, like rawhide, could be too large and cause him to choke.

Dogs in your pack are great teachers and caretakers for your new pup.

Older pets may not be as tolerant of active pups. Create a quiet retreat away from the puppy's domain where your older pet can rest.

Submissive peeing is not unusual. Be tolerant of this behavior. If you don't make a big deal out of it or ignore it, the behavior will eventually correct itself as your puppy grows older and more confident.

Walks with Duffy

Corrie was our salvation. Duffy mellowed with this puppy. Jingles found a new puppy annoying so she spent most of her days away from home, even as we worried for her safety with coyotes prowling the canyons.

Duffy was Corrie's personal play toy, but even he couldn't keep up with her energy. She kept Duffy hopping and entertained him more than we could anymore. In hindsight, we wondered why we rejected the idea of having a puppy sooner. Most likely, we were afraid of a repeat of extreme behavior with another Aussie.

Because of her, Duffy tolerated other dogs better. We still couldn't trust him, but he stopped lunging at dogs when Corrie stood nearby.

When I finally got my sister, we walked far together. Everybody wanted to meet Corrie. Because she's cute! Just like me. Corrie peed on everybody. Embarrassing. Can't be alpha dog if you pee. Mama said she's a Princess. I guess you can pee on humans if you're a Princess.

We met a lot of humans and new dogs. I made sure they stayed far. Some dogs were bad. One dog tried to eat her. I gave him what for before Daddy could stop me. That dog stayed far now. Corrie needed to learn. I protected her from those. She watched for signals now. Not everybody's friendly. She ran behind me when she's scared. At least she didn't pee on me anymore. Embarrassing. Can't be brave if you pee all the time.

There's a couple dogs like us on our estate. Mama said we're relatives. I don't know relatives, but they smelled like us. One is Kai. He reminded me of Katie. White and black all mixed up. Wrapper is just like me. Big boy, but nice. Knew his place. Corrie liked him, but not as much as she liked me.

We met another relative at the Pet Store. Lots bigger than me. His mama stopped to play with Corrie. I flew by but Daddy's quick this time, so I'm stuck. His mama said Jafar was 86 pounds. He got a lot of cookies. Lots! I could tell. Just like Lee's sausage terriers, Rusty and Dusty. Lee must be their neighbor.

 TIP:

Your puppy can also be a great influence on your other pets. Observe their interactions to see how they teach each other.

Training My Puppy

Housebreaking Corrie was a lot harder than Duffy. He seemed to learn everything in one try. We endured her submissive peeing when she met new people or if she was overjoyed at a new experience. We now had Nature's Miracle in big jugs as well as spray bottles.

After years of suffering Duffy's frantic behavior in the car, we decided Corrie would learn how to ride without the drama. She delighted us by being an excellent passenger.

We also learned about a leash called the Gentle Leader and promptly bought one for Corrie. It made walks a lot easier without the pulling and tugging, but she still managed to pick up awful things discarded on the road.

The hardest command for her was "drop it." She was defiant, but definitely not as headstrong as Duffy. We were grateful for that, but the learning process wasn't always easy.

Corrie was a good puppy. Not too smart, but good. She still peed on everybody. Daddy took to the bottle of "thank heaven for Nature's Miracle" every day now. I guess he liked a wet floor. And house grass. Her pee door didn't work good when she got excited.

Mama took us for rides around the block. I was worried. I thought we were going to take my puppy back, but she's safe. Mama said no noise allowed so we're quiet. I'm brave now and didn't say anything. I stuck my nose out the window. Corrie didn't get a window. Mama put her in a crate. Mama said I have to set an example. Am I going to be Corrie's vet? The Vet did my exams.

Mama and Daddy got Corrie a face dress. They called it Gentle Leader. Mama said she walked better with it. I don't get it. Corrie's face didn't walk, but her paws worked good. My parents are so confused.

Mama doesn't like the stuff Corrie picks up. One day Mama put her whole paw in Corrie's mouth. To go fishing. Corrie gagged. No fish came out, but Mama said it was disgusting all the same. "Yuck, it's a cigarette butt!" Didn't know cigarette. Too bad. Cigarette can't sit down anymore.

Daddy gave Corrie pine cones to carry. She drooled all over it. I told her it's undignified. She didn't listen. She carried one every day all over our estate.

A baby gave her a ball one day. Mama and Daddy wanted her to give it back. Uh-uh. Her toy. I told her let go. Uh-uh. Brave. We walked all the way home with it. Mama gave her what for when we got home. Daddy said, "Oh, just let her have it." Mama said, "No! She has to learn!" Corrie growled and Mama barked until Corrie let go. Loud. Real loud. Lots of barking. Growling. Lots of "give" then a real loud "Drop it." Daddy and I stayed far. Not that brave. Ball came out.

Corrie said, "Bubby, what happened?" I said, you better give when Mama says give. "Drop it" means Death. I told Corrie to learn fast. I didn't want them to kill her.

Corrie loved her treats more than me. She cleaned up all my crumbs. Mama was so happy. No crumbs. Just tongue tracks. I told Corrie we had more, but she didn't know yet. She liked to make Mama happy. She got to sit in Daddy's lap when he was in the "hell to pay" chair. Not me. I liked Mama's chair better. Mama didn't bark when I sat there. She knew I'm the king. Corrie knew too. It's my chair. Even Mama sat on the floor sometimes. I let Mama sit on her chair a lot, though. She needed it more than me.

🐾 **TIPS:**

Never forcefully remove an object from your dog's mouth. Divert his attention with something of higher value, like a cookie or toy, so he'll release the object you want. Praise him when he lets go.

Teach your dog to release or leave a toy or object on command.

Playing tug with your new pup is fun, but you need to train him on the limits of that game. The heightened excitement could lead to aggression.

Rabies Shot

When it was time to get Corrie a rabies shot, Duffy seemed to sense this outing would be a big event. His behavior stressed Corrie a lot, but we all managed to make the visit fairly painless. We found taking them to the vet separately, though inconvenient, made the visits a lot easier. At least he couldn't influence Corrie by his frenzied behavior.

My parents took Corrie to the Vet to get shot. Daddy said I scared the Vet last time so I didn't go. He scared me so much I didn't notice. I told her, "Fight hard if they throw you upside down on the table." She said she was ready to run if they did. The Vet got a Bumble Bee to sting her in the back instead. They shot her rabies. I guess it's good to shoot rabies. Everybody was nice to her, but Corrie knew a Bumble Bee was coming. I guess she's not stupid after all.

Corrie didn't understand why the Vet was so mean. She said they fool you by being nice, and then they shoot you. I didn't get it either. Mama said, "So you don't get sick." I never got sick so why did I get shot? They're confused. Like the time I got bad treats because the other dog had a cough. I tried to explain to Corrie, but she didn't get it. Some things will never make sense.

Corrie's Surgery

We decided to have Corrie spayed when she was six months old. She had her dinner the night before, and then fasted until we dropped her off early in the morning. Duffy was very insistent on going with us even though Bernard filled his breakfast bowl with meaty morsels to distract him. Corrie was off to the vet. Neither of them understood what was happening.

At the end of the day, we picked up Corrie. She was groggy and sore. Duffy met us at the door. His concern overshadowed his happiness at her return. He whined as he sniffed her all over to make sure she was okay. Even though she happily greeted him, he was so stressed he guarded her carefully and drooled for over a half-hour after her return.

My parents kidnapped my sister in SUV this morning. She's not so smart. I knew something was fishy. She was hungry, but didn't smell any fish. She's going to the Vet. I know. I've been around the block a few times. Daddy never went with Mama and me or Corrie anywhere. It's the Vet! I know. I smelled fish.

I tried to block them when they put Corrie in SUV. Daddy said, "Get out of the way!" Not the way! Uh-uh. I'm smart. I know better. The Vet is going to sting her with Bumble Bees. Lots.

Mama was whining a little when she came home. Daddy was sad too. What happened to my sister? Did the Vet shoot her? Oh, no! I whined too. She's too young to die! Waah! Rooo!! Mama said Corrie's having surgery. At the Vet. I don't like the Vet's house. I had surgery where I sit down. Never going back. Uh-uh. No way!

Mama called the Vet all day. I think the Vet got lost. I hoped they fed Corrie. She's a little girl and needed to eat. Mama and Daddy starved her today. We waited and waited. Nobody called. Mama called again. Finally, the Vet called back. Late. Real late. Dinner time. Not hungry. My sister is lost.

Mama and Daddy left me home. I didn't care. I missed my sister. Lying near her crate. Her smell made me feel better. I fell asleep. I hoped they went to look for my sister. I waited a long time. Long. I heard my sister crying. Scared. Hurt. I thought I was dreaming at first.

SUV coming home. I yipped a lot. Rooo! I smelled my sister. Rooo! She's home! Corrie doesn't look so good. She whined a lot. Her head was in a big can. Like my e-collar a long time ago. Must be why she couldn't come home. She walked funny. Can must be heavy. Her paws didn't work right. Wobbly. I licked her face and she fell down. Cried when she did. No, no! Corrie had surgery where she sits down too! Mean! Mama and Daddy are mean! The Vet is mean! I'm mad. Not fair. We sat down fine before. Waaah! Rooo! I whined a lot.

Mama said, "It's okay."

I knew better. Not okay. I hoped they put all her stuffing back in.

Mama took her to the backyard. Corrie had to pee. Long time. Long. She walked real slow in the house. Mama had to carry her. She smelled bad. I tried to find out why, but Mama pushed me away. Not nice. She told me not to play with Corrie because she's sore. I know that. I heard her crying long before they got home. It made my heart hurt.

When Mama and Daddy didn't look, I licked her face. She didn't see too good, but licked me too. Slow tongue. Sleepy. I laid next to her until dinner. She ate a lot. Went back to sleep. I stayed. Licked her when she whined. My little sister. I loved her a lot. Nobody will take her away again. I hope they ate the Vet.

🐾 **TIP:**

Spaying and neutering, though seemingly barbaric to some, helps prevent potential health problems later in your dog's life. If your puppy will be a family pet, this procedure should be considered as a means of limiting unwanted puppies and dogs that overburden shelters every day.

Corrie Goes to Obedience School

Corrie was old enough now for obedience lessons. I found a new school through an obedience club and hoped they could teach me better than our first trainer. Bernard had enough of training with Duffy so he said with a laugh, "Have fun! We'll be here when you get home. Good luck!"

"Gee, thanks," I thought.

The club paperwork stated we should take a hot dog and cut it into 250 pieces for the training, so I dutifully cut a hot dog as directed and put it in a plastic bag. By the end of the first lesson, I realized I needed a small towel to wipe the grease from the hot dog off my fingers and a third hand to hold a clicker. Since no third hand was imminent, I dispensed with the clicker.

The Gentle Leader we bought minimized the excited pulling she learned from Duffy. It actually worked! Corrie pulled, but I was able to control her without having my arm torn out of its socket.

Corrie's training went a lot better than Duffy's, although she didn't have the patience to wait for other dogs to get their turns either. She was unhappy sitting still. It frustrated me to have her frantically paw and jump on me while we waited for other dogs to get their turns. At least she didn't howl or bark like Duffy. After our first six weeks, the trainer invited us back to continue with lessons. What a relief not to be unceremoniously thrown out!

We took one more series of lessons before I decided to work with her on my own. I also searched for other activities that might drain her boundless energy. We realized the hyperactivity was not an anomaly with Duffy. It was a common breed trait! I guess we'll be in for another wild ride.

Whee! Rooo! Not me this time! I didn't have to go because I'm smart. I told Corrie to listen good or Daddy would throw her on a table and a Bumble Bee would bite her leg. For her Eye-Dee so she won't get lost. Corrie asked, "Who's lost?" I said, "Mama and Daddy." They have no idea.

She must be a good girl because they didn't throw her on the table. She didn't like school because she had to wear her face dress. She didn't like her dress. Mama would pull and she ended up looking at herself. I think flybys and flybacks were better. Even choking. The only thing she liked was the hotdog. Yum! I love hotdogs. My favorite. None for me or Daddy, though. I had to wear my dress to get those hotdogs. I'd rather be naked at home. Wild life is being naked.

After graduation, they told Mama to come back. I guess Corrie is stupid after all. Corrie was mad because she didn't like school. She said she did what Mama wanted, but had to do it again. She only got a tiny hotdog for it. Tiny. Cheap! I told her Mama didn't learn so fast. She had to go until Mama got trained. Corrie sat down and listened, but she still didn't like school.

Corrie learned to bark in the car. When they got to school. Bad. She didn't think it was bad. All the dogs barked there. Mama was barking loud too. I said listen to how she barks. Mama's mad bark was different. Corrie said Mama was barking "shut up" and "quiet" and banging on her crate. A lot. Must be her mad bark. Mama's mad bark is scary. Then she'd take her to the Vet again. I know. I had experience. Lots.

🐾 **TIPS:**

When training your dog, give him small pieces of treats. He doesn't need a whole cookie or a large bite of hotdog to feel rewarded. A taste is all that is needed. When you spend a lot of time training your dog, keeping his weight stable is important.

Use a clicker to train your dog. It helps to "mark" the desired behavior and reinforce what you are trying to teach.

Select a leash that's right for you and your dog.

Corrie and the Kitty

Jingles didn't linger outside once she returned home from a night's foraging anymore. She encountered several neighborhood cats intent on claiming territory, and her loud hisses and yowls would bring Duffy headlong into the fray. He never got hurt, but it scared us to think how dangerous it could be for him. He was twelve years old, still fast, but not as agile as before.

A new kitten also appeared in our yard. It was a pretty little feline with orange stripes and bright green eyes. Her beauty belied her fearsome attitude. She would hide in the shrubs and pounce out at anyone who came nearby with a hiss and yowl so loud it was startling. One morning, Corrie ran around the perimeter of the yard for her morning inspection when this kitten jumped out at her. She was so surprised by the sight and sound that she screamed and flew back to us for protection. I had to admit that I was startled by the ferocity of this little cat too. Duffy barked wildly and ran at her as she leapt over the fence and disappeared. He came back with a big grin on his face. We all laughed about it as well, after we got over her fierce confrontation.

This kitty returned a few times, still asserting herself when she did. Eventually, she stopped coming by. She challenged a larger cat once and might have been chased away or taken by the wildlife. She was a formidable foe!

A new Kitty was in the yard today. I saw it first, but Corrie ran to check it out. Her first Kitty. I tried to call her back. Kitty was hiding. Scared. Didn't like us. I could smell it. Not just scared, though. Mean scared.

Corrie ran up quick. She thought it was a puppy. Maybe her missing sister or brother. No! Too late. Kitty jumped at her and said bad things. Loud bad things. Corrie screamed, "Eeeeeek! Eeek! Bubby! Eeek!" and ran behind me. Afraid. I showed her how to handle a kitty. I went to Kitty's hiding place and barked. A lot. She ran and jumped over the fence. I told Corrie that's how you gave what for.

Next day, Kitty was back. Corrie was sneaky this time. Kitty ran away. Good. Corrie learned fast. She sniffed and came back happy. She said she gave her first what for! One more day and Corrie forgot. She ran and sniffed around the yard without looking. Kitty jumped out and screamed something real mean. Made me jump too. Corrie screamed loud and ran back to me.

I laughed to myself. "Told you! Sneak!" We both sneak. Corrie behind me. Way behind. Tongue leaking. Whining. Afraid to get too close. Kitty jumped out and said the bad thing to me too. I jumped and growled. Bark! Growl! We ran around fast. Kitty jumped on the fence. Too bad. This was fun! Corrie's happy again. Not afraid to bark now. She learned to give what for. She snuck to Kitty's hiding place and sniffed to make sure she was gone. Safe for now.

We played this game for a long time. Long. At least two weeks. Kitty disappeared after that. A big cat and Kitty got in a fight. Mama said big cat chased our Kitty away. Too bad. We needed a new toy to chase. No bunnies yet. Corrie liked to chase too. Mama and Daddy threw balls for us. We chased together. She ran faster than me. Almost like McKenzie, but Corrie's small. Just a puppy. But fast. Real fast. I ran a few times, but my paw hurt again. Hurt from when I was a puppy. I let her play with Mama.

🐾 **TIP:**

Cats can be very dangerous foes to unwary dogs. Unless you and your dog know the cat, don't allow him to confront one. Cat scratches can cause nasty infections or serious injury to your dog.

Grooming

I didn't groom Duffy regularly until he was about seven years old. I brushed him after his baths from the start, but didn't learn how to keep knots out of his coat so he often looked raggedy. Once I started trimming his knots, I experimented on the rest of his body, particularly his back end. During the summer, I'd give him a butt bob.

We had an awful experience with his toenails so I avoided that job as long as I could. His nails stayed filed down most of the time from the strenuous pulling during his walks.

Duffy was a pro about his grooming now. He let me snip away without a backward glance. For Corrie, this was all new, but I was determined to teach her to accept the spa treatments as something good and fun.

I told Corrie all about Mama's weapons. She got scared and hid under my face. She needed to learn fast. She had to know what's coming when she got older. I told her Mama and Daddy are nice at first. Once the baths start, nice time is over. You can shake all you want, but Towel was the best. Make sure you roll on it. A lot. Don't roll in the dirt or mud. Mama got mad when you did that. Real mad! Second bath mad. So let the good times roll. After that, it's all downhill.

 TIPS*:

Teach your dog about grooming at an early age.

Bathe him regularly.

More brushing may mean less baths.

Learn to trim your dog's nails or monitor their growth. Have someone clip them for you when they get long.

Your dog needs dental care.

*These tips are mentioned in an earlier chapter.

Corrie's First Holiday

Corrie's first experience with fireworks was the Fourth of July. Since we had ringside seats to the wonderful fireworks, we let her and Duffy sit on the bed to watch with us. Bernard pulled away the blinds so we could look out through our large bedroom window. Corrie was enthralled by all the noise and lights, unlike Duffy who year after year hyperventilated and drooled in the closet through the show. He didn't run out or try to hide this time, which was unusual for him. I couldn't tell if he was putting on a brave front for Corrie or just getting used to the noise after all these years.

Corrie got to watch the fireworks with us this year. On the bed. I was shaking, but didn't want to leave Corrie. Mama opened the big window so we could see. Corrie liked the pretty lights and got up every time it got bright. She tried to play with me. "Look, Bubby!" Then she jumped on me until I did. Afraid. I had to be brave. Can't have her think her Bubby is a big baby. My tongue was leaking, but I tried. Leaking. All over the bed. Good thing she didn't know I was scared. She made me brave. I didn't die after all.

 TIPS:

Behaviors or fears that you don't know how to correct may be a simple fix when your dog observes another dog ignoring the troubling situation.

Reinforce his courage at facing his fears with treats.

Corrie Likes Cat Food

Duffy finally got his chance to teach Corrie about cat food. Bernard thought the coast was clear when he opened the door. As soon as his back was turned, Duffy and Corrie ran in. Duffy inhaled deeply from Jingles' bowl with little Corrie right behind. Between the two of them, half the bowl of food was eaten before Bernard could get them out. What sneaky little devils they are! Duffy's teaching Corrie his bad habits.

I taught Corrie how to hunt for cat food. Corrie and I got to Jingles' food when Daddy was slow. Yum! Daddy was mad! He said I sucked it up like a vacuum. I didn't whine like the Vacuum, though. Noisy. Vacuum hurt my ears so I chased and barked at it until it stopped whining. Gourmet food all gone! Too bad. Daddy has to get his own. I saved a little for Corrie. She said, "Bubby, it's good!" Got to be fast, though. Fast! We hung around Jingles' room all the time when Daddy went in. Corrie liked fast food.

No Surfing

Duffy never clawed or climbed on people or furniture in quest for food. It was beneath his dignity to beg. Instead, he waited quietly for special morsels he knew would come his way. Not so his little sister. She wanted to see everything. After many attempts to stop her counter surfing by pushing her away or saying "off," a friend told me to step on her toes—not hard, but enough to remember. After she attempted to surf on the stove top when Bernard was cooking, we decided it was time for drastic action. A couple of tries later, she seemed to get the message.

Corrie liked to stand up near the table or counter. Mama and Daddy didn't like that. They called it counter surfing. Didn't know Surfing, but I knew begging was undignified. No couth! Mama and Daddy barked at her when she did. A lot. One day, Mama stepped on her toes. She yiked and ran to me. I told her, "No, no bad!"

"But, Bubby, I wanted to see!"

You'll see better when you sit and wait. Otherwise, they'll eat your toes.

She forgot a couple times but learned to stop surfing. After that, Corrie sat even though she wanted to look. Her toes remembered.

🐾 TIP:

Teaching your dog not to jump on people, your table, or counter can be exasperating. Stepping on your dog's toes may hurt him. Instead, put his leash on him and step on the leash when he attempts to jump. This will inhibit the distance he can elevate himself while you teach him not to jump.

Chapter 18

Farewell

Jingles Is Gone

We didn't worry about Jingles' evening escapades so much anymore. She managed to stay out of harm's way for five years in our new neighborhood. We estimated she was approaching twenty years of age now.

Bernard and I noticed she was slowing down. Duffy would intervene whenever she needed help fighting off other cats who ventured in our yard. She still fed herself well enough and came home just to eat a few bites of her kibble before she took her daytime nap in her safe room.

Eventually, several days passed without her leaving the house. That's when we noticed her behavior bordered on bizarre. More often than not, she would yowl and cry in fear if we approached her. She didn't always recognize Bernard, her main caretaker. She hid in her safe room alone, but cowered in the corner and occasionally forgot how to use her litter box. Bernard thought she had dementia.

One fateful day, Jingles left and never returned. We waited several days before searching for her, but we never saw her again.

Jingles wasn't feeling so good. Tired a lot. We looked at each other. We understood. We've been around the block a few times. She rubbed my face like when I was a puppy. Still stinky. But that's okay. Just this time.

Jingles said she's tired and scared all the time. Cried a lot. Old. Tired. Too many scary things. One too many fights. Couldn't hear or see so good. Too many shadows. Everything jumped out at her. I had to chase cats away for her. Too hard, especially with a puppy not smart about cats yet. Corrie got in the way. She didn't see danger. Jingles said she's leaving soon but wanted to say good-bye.

Corrie didn't understand. She just wanted to play. Jingles moved slow. Me too, but I had a lot of work left to do. I told Corrie she had to learn fast now. Even if she's a girl.

One day, Jingles didn't come home. She was real old. Old. At least two tens. Not today. Not tomorrow either. We waited for a long time. Long. Daddy and Mama looked around the neighborhood. Couldn't call her. Too stupid to know her name. Even at home she cried when we got close. Daddy said she had dementia. I didn't see anybody new. Daddy said, "Jingles doesn't know me anymore." She was afraid all the time. Sometimes afraid of me too. Her brains must be shrinking.

Daddy said she missed her little box all the time. I don't get it. It's still in the room. It's Dementia making the mess. Stinky. Real stinky. I tried to sneak in to be sure, but Daddy pushed me away. Even Corrie couldn't get in. She knew there's fast food in there, but we're locked out.

Mama and Daddy waited a real long time. Long. At least two weeks. No Jingles. My parents were sad. They told Corrie and me, "Jingles went to college, so we won't see her anymore." I didn't believe it. She must be somewhere else. Jingles wasn't smart enough for college. Maybe Cat College. Didn't need to be smart to get there. Maybe she found someplace better to eat and sleep. And no fights. Too many cats around here now. She couldn't give what for like she used to. And hard with a puppy around who wanted to play all the time. Too tired for that when she only wanted to sleep. That's okay. We could finish her food. Except the rats. Eww! Disgusting!

So no more cat food or little box for us. Daddy took it to Jingles' new home at Cat College. Wherever that is, I hoped she liked it better. Maybe she'll meet somebody like me. Somebody to save her. Her and Dementia.

Not Feeling Good

I watched an animal rescue program on Animal Planet. The vet examined a dog who had been riddled with ticks and fleas. The dog's gums were very pale. I decided to check Duffy's gums as well and, to my horror, his gums were pale too. I told Bernard we needed to take him for a checkup.

Bernard said, "Don't get paranoid over a TV show." Ever since Duffy turned ten, I watched for every odd change in his health. Yes, I may have been paranoid, but I had to be sure he was fine.

The vet took a blood sample, even though he wasn't convinced Duffy had a health problem. The vet sent out the sample to the University of California-Davis lab. The results showed his white blood cell count was elevated and there were signs of anemia.

All of a sudden, there was an urgency to do more tests with an oncologist. Then a biopsy. Duffy had a mass in his liver.

I'm slowing down now. Something heavy inside. Couldn't run and jump like I used to. Hard to keep up with Corrie. I needed to teach her fast now. I knew something's inside. Like I ate a ball, but I didn't remember.

One day Mama was watching TV. A dog on it had bad gums. I had bad gum once. Yummy going in, but bad coming out. Mama pulled my face up to see inside and told Daddy I need to see The

V-E-T. Oh, no! The Vet! I know V-E-T. They thought I couldn't spell, but I'm smart. Mama and Daddy thought they fooled me, but I know. That's the Vet! I'm afraid, but too sore to fuss.

The next day we went to the Vet's house. He poked me with a big Bumble Bee, but I went home right after. After my cookie. The Vet needed better cookies. Mama said we could wait for the results at home. Good. I didn't like the Vet's house. Everybody's scared. I got the Bumble Bee again.

Mama said I needed to take a test. Not worried. I'm smart. They said it was a biopsy. I don't know Opsy, but I'm good at any test. Even if it's by Opsy. I had to go to the Vet's house again. Only this time I had a new Vet. Mama said she's a specialist. She's my New Vet because I'm special. I knew that!

She smelled nice, but everybody else was scared. Tried to fool me. Mama and Daddy let them take me away. I heard "sleep" and "stay" and "tomorrow." Wait! I've been around the block a few times. That means my parents are leaving me. No! I'm a good boy! They didn't want me because I'm sick and I had a good sister now. Waah! Rooo!

I slept for a long time. Long. When I got up, it was hard to breathe. I hurt when I moved. Couldn't wake up. Sleepy. For days! Corrie licked my face. I hurt so I didn't lick back. She's sad. She stayed close to me. Too hurt to move. She brought me toys. I couldn't play. Just wanted to sleep and make the hurt go away.

The devastating news was in. Duffy had liver cancer. The disease had metastasized. The oncologist said he might have four months. How can this be? He was fine, now he isn't.

The biopsy caused Duffy so much agony we wished we hadn't put him through it. Every day I hoped he'd spring back to his old self, but he never did.

I heard Mama crying today. She's sad. Real sad. Sadder than ever. Even after Popo and Gramee got lost. She told Daddy I had liver cancer. Yum! I liked liver. Liver's my favorite! They're going to give me some in a can. I could eat from a can, but I liked my bowl better. I sniffed, but didn't smell any. I told Corrie to look for liver cans. We waited, but no liver came. Too bad.

I got a new treat, though. Cottage cheese! Yum! Good. Especially the cottages. Corrie liked it too. When we licked the spoon, the cottages flew all over. We tried to save some for dinner later. Cottages made my tummy feel better, but the ball was still there. I didn't like to think about the ball.

Daddy and Mama talked in secret. Big words I didn't understand. Metas-something. Then Mama cried again. Daddy's sad too. I'm too tired to listen.

I taught Corrie fast now. No time to waste. I didn't hurt so bad, but the ball is still there. Heavy. It's time for me to go to college. I worried. I couldn't eat too good. Couldn't walk too far. Better to just sleep. I felt sick all the time. Vet's boo shots didn't work anymore.

I got lots of hugs and kisses from Mama after that. Corrie too. She didn't know why, but she watched and learned. She's a good girl.

🐾 TIPS:

Be watchful of changes in your dog's physical condition.

Grooming helps you to discover anomalies on his skin, paws, ears, and mouth.

Annual checkups should be an integral part of his health routine.

You may not be able to discover or prevent some illnesses, but do what you are able to ensure a long, happy, healthy life for your pet.

Last Battle

Duffy had difficult days after his diagnosis. He didn't go for long walks anymore. Short trips around the block were all he could handle.

Our neighbors' gardener left the back gate open one day when Bernard and Duffy headed out for their walk. Their two dogs attacked Duffy and Bernard on the street. Bernard crouched over to protect Duffy from harm. I heard the commotion and ran out to see what was happening. Two men and a woman stood nearby but did nothing. I yelled as loud as I could to the dogs to "go home!" Luckily, they snapped out of their attack and ran back behind their gate.

I was livid that no one tried to help! My poor, sick Duffy! My poor Bernard!

Daddy and I went for a walk. Just him and me. Corrie was with Mama. Two bad dogs got out of their yard. Cammi and Bear ran after us to pick a fight. I tried to fight, but not strong anymore. Not afraid, just tired. They knew. Daddy saved me. He jumped in the middle and held me. Mama came out and barked and growled at them until they went home. She barked real loud. Loud! Almost as loud as my bad bath day long ago. She growled so loud, Cammi and Bear ran home to hide. They're smart to stay far. Some humans came out to watch. Mama was mad at them too. She said something like "worthless" and "frozen." Mad! Nobody helped Daddy. She was still barking and growling all the way home. I tried to protect our estate, but Daddy had to do it that day.

I had a hole on my head and Daddy hurt his paw, but he was okay after. Just a bite. It's a sad day to be like Jingles. No fight left. Tried. Failed.

Mama's so mad she wrote a letter to the neighbor. They whined at us later so Mama felt better. My head hurt, but Daddy's paw hurt worse. He told Mama, "My thumb got crunched." I don't know Thumb so I don't know how bad it felt. Must be worse than my head hole. No brains came out so I'm still smart. Corrie came to check. She tried to lick my head hole, but I just wanted to sleep.

I knew it was time for me to finish teaching my puppy everything I could. The days were getting short. Corrie needed me. Too much for her to learn on her own. I had to get as many rules together as I could.

Final Instructions

We could see Duffy fading more and more each day. Corrie stayed close by as if she knew he would be leaving us soon. She licked him several times each day, presumably to say she loved him. He was so good to her. We saw how much he influenced her behavior, and we were sorry to see him go so soon. We just didn't know if Duffy had enough time to make a long-lasting impact.

My mama said I'm a genius and will go to college soon. I knew already. I felt bad now. Real bad. I didn't know if I could make the trip. It's a long away. Far. Way past the park she said. My ball hurt when I walked. Especially after the Vet. I fell asleep and didn't see what happened. I still wanted to sleep. Daddy gave me some gourmet food. He said I would feel better. I tried. It's good, but my ball hurt. Still no liver. I had the urpies and poopies a lot. Embarrassing. No couth. Too tired to care.

In the mornings, I woke up and smelled the roses. The trees and yard too, but mostly the roses. If you got too close, they poked like the Bumble Bee, but they smelled nice. I didn't feel good so nice made me feel better. Corrie followed me, but she didn't stop to smell the roses. Too much going on. She chased a bird out of the yard. Barked too. Good. She's learning to guard her estate. Best I could teach her. She had to remember everything. Couldn't help her much now.

I taught Corrie every day. I reminded her to be a good girl and remember the rules.

Number one: No surfing! Mama and Daddy don't like paws on the table or counter. Undignified. Be couth! "Bubby, I get excited and forget myself sometimes." I reminded her about her toes. It didn't come easy with a puppy. Small brains. Especially girls.

Number two: No picking up disgusting things. Mama will go fishing and pull out your stuffing. Make you gag. Mama did that to me a lot when I was a puppy. If she doesn't get it, then you get the blues and Mama has to fish behind your rootie-toot. Embarrassing. Or worse, you get a bath. "Bubby, I don't like baths." Then don't do it.

Number three: Remember to "give" when Mama says give. "Drop it" means Death. "Bubby, I don't want to die. Will they kill me when I die?" Don't know. They haven't killed me yet. If they do, you'll know.

Number four: No flybys with Mama. She can't pull tight like Daddy. If you walk with Daddy, you're a goner. "Bubby, my face dress isn't good for flybys." Good. Safer for you.

Number five: No jumping or peeing on humans. It's fun, but they don't like it. "Bubby, I forget and can't stop!" Try. It's embarrassing to be weak. Peeing on humans and dogs is weak. Mama wants humans to like you. Have to control yourself or they take your friends away. Like mine when I was a puppy. I suffered because I had to guard the estate. Because I'm the king. It's my job. Hard to be number one. If you're good, Mama will let you have friends. You're number one now. Have to be brave, but be nice too. Mama will take you to see lots of fun places and you can have friends if you're nice. Not like me. I had to be strong all the time because I'm king. Be brave, even if you get scared. You have to protect your estate. No matter what. I showed you how to give what for. "I'll try, Bubby. Even if the kitty comes back." Good. It's your estate now.

Number six: Go riding with Mama. She can take you places I never saw when I was a puppy. Don't be scared like I was. No couth. Not so scary to ride SUV now. Trouble is long gone. Lost forever. Good. You can have lots of friends because you go with Mama. "Bubby, you're my best friend!"

Number seven: Make Mama and Daddy play outside. A lot. The house isn't as fun, but they don't get it. "Oh, Bubby, I like that!

Especially with my balls and toys!" Yeah, we have lots of toys. Make sure you use them all so they don't forget.

Number eight: Let Mama put you in her lap. And put stuff on you, like a hat. "Bubby, I don't like that! I bite to get free!" I know. Me too, but she likes it. It makes her happy. Don't bite. That's worse than Death. She might kill you for sure. You have to sacrifice to make humans happy.

Number nine: Mama's the boss now. Daddy too. Listen to them like you listen to me. "But, Bubby, sometimes I don't understand." Don't worry. You'll get smart soon. Maybe not smart like me but good enough. It didn't take me long.

Number ten: Don't be scared of the Vet. Sometimes they shoot you with the Bumble Bee, but most times it doesn't hurt long. You get more cookies if you're brave. "Bubby, the Vet's house smells bad and they do bad things to me. I get scared a lot. But, I'll try." Try.

Remember that I love you. Your Mama and Daddy love you too. I was always scared they would be mean to me. They never were. Because they loved me. I know how much now.

Going to College

I never thought of Duffy's passing as dying. I liked to think he was going to college, because he was so smart. Heaven would not have been a happy place for him. Flying around with a harp and lying on fluffy white clouds didn't suit him. He needed something or someplace to stimulate his mind. He needed a job! Where better to prepare than in college?

Bernard and I loved Duffy equally, but it was doubly unbearable for me to let him go. He was, for lack of a better definition, my child. His energy dwindled now and he couldn't keep his food down. We knew it was almost time.

Corrie wanted to come with me. I told her she's not smart enough yet. If ever. She had to stay with Mama and Daddy until she's smart. She'd better listen to me and learn fast or she may never go to college. She was sad but said she'd try. Mama and Daddy wouldn't let her jump on me and puppy play now. Because my ball hurt. Bad. I think Corrie knew too. She was real nice to me and kissed me a lot. Soggy, but I don't mind. It made me think of my mom.

Carolyn's husband, Roy, had been chronically ill for a long time. She also realized his recent trip to the hospital was different. Little did we know their candles would flicker out almost simultaneously.

Uncle Roy didn't feel good either. Mama and Auntie Carolyn were both sad. He knew it was a long trip to college. He was in bed a lot. Resting up. Just like me. Auntie Carolyn said he was a professor. He used to live at college. I hoped we could make the trip together so I wouldn't get lost. He could kidnap me if he wanted. I won't cry this time. I knew he wouldn't eat me. He's a vegetarian. I could find termite trees for us to eat if we got hungry.

I heard Mama and Daddy talking. They said it wouldn't be long now. I was sick all night. Daddy kept me company so I wouldn't cry. He knew this was a hard trip. He went to college too. Only in Hawaii. He could fly too. At least three blocks. I wished I could fly. Maybe it's not so far if I could fly.

Mama and Daddy can't come to college with me. I have to go alone. Nobody to take care of Corrie if they did. Not enough time to teach her everything so Mama and Daddy have to take over.

Daddy said we had to make one last trip in SUV. Corrie can't come. We said good-bye at home. Corrie licked me a lot. My face was soggy again. Just like with my mom. I licked her once. Remember what I taught you. "Bubby, don't go! Waaah!" She tried to follow, but Mama and Daddy put her in her crate. I heard her crying, "Don't go! B-b-ub-bee!" but I needed to go. I sat on the Car Pet. We're all quiet now. Never did figure out what Car Pet did. Just kept us company I guess. I'll have to ask in college.

We passed my old estate and I said good-bye to my friends at the park, even though I couldn't see them. I knew they heard me. Katie, Rusty, Dusty, Ricky, McKenzie, Sassy, Scarlett, even Ginger. I heard Dan and Lee too, with her box of cookies. Yum! All there.

I hung my face out the window and my tongue was leaking. It felt good even though my ball hurt. Mama and Daddy were real sad. Sad. Their hearts hurt. Mine too. Going to college was hard.

My parents tried, but they ran out of new stuff to teach me. I'm a genius, so they had to let me go. I felt bad. I'll miss them. A lot. I didn't know how long I had to be in college. Maybe Uncle Roy will tell me. I hoped he and I could go together. Mama said he could show me the ropes. I liked ropes. I ate them all the time. Gotta be careful, though. Big ones fight back.

We stopped to see the Vet. They're sad to see me there. They all kissed me, and I put on my brave face. I didn't want to cry. Mama and Daddy kissed me a lot too. Especially Mama. She loved me most. Even more than Corrie. I could tell. Because I'm smart. Even the Bumble Bee came to say good-bye. I closed my eyes. Sleepy.

I heard Uncle Roy. He said he's leaving soon. "Wait for me at the Rainbow Bridge. It's not far. You'll know it when you get there. Then we'll go to college together."

It's real pretty here. Especially the rainbow. I'm not hungry, but the grass is good. My ball is gone and I don't hurt anymore. I run through the big fields. My paw doesn't hurt either. Yum! I love grass. Grass is my favorite. Uncle Roy will probably like it too. He's a vegetarian. I miss Mama and Daddy already. They told me they loved me and will miss me with all their hearts. They cried a lot before I left. They promised to take care of Corrie for me. She's in good hands now. I taught my parents a lot since I was a puppy. But they'll all see me someday. When they get smart enough for college too. Even my stupid sister if she can make it to Cat College. I'm happy now.

Epilogue

After all the lessons Duffy taught us, Corrie became a shining star. She was a beautiful dog with the sweetest personality. People were drawn to her. We made so many wonderful friendships with neighbors, colleagues, and fellow canine lovers and competitors because she initiated the introductions.

Corrie performed in agility and obedience, garnering eighty-six titles and two championships in her competitive career. She stepped into the Australian Shepherd Club of America's San Diego show rings occasionally, but just for fun. We couldn't have asked for a better dog!

Duffy had a huge impact on her life, even though they only spent six months together. They created a bond that lasted long after he departed for the Rainbow Bridge.

"Nothing is ever lost in this adventure of all adventures. The lessons and discoveries of every single life, no matter how large or small, difficult or easy, are added to the whole. Like stones in the base of a pyramid, they permanently raise, and forever support every manner of adventure that follows. And so it is that the hearts of those who came first continue to beat in all subsequent generations, forevermore. *Every single life.*"

—Mike Dooley from *More Notes from the Universe*

About the Author

Faith McCune's first dog was a gift from her mother after her father passed away. She was eight at the time and Prince helped her cope with her loss and brought joy into her heart again. Prince was her best friend and confidante. Her passion for dogs was forged from her first dog and grew over the decades with each new dog she raised.

Faith is an author and founder of Duffy's World Inc., a place where dog owners and dog lovers gather to share and learn more about their furry companions. She encourages people to seek greater understanding of dogs and their behaviors to assure happy "forever" homes for pets and their owners. Faith believes that if you open your heart to a dog, you will reawaken the joy in your own life.

Duffy's cautionary tale speaks of how love through the best of times and worst of challenges can produce the most amazing results—if not completely for him, the next one who comes along. Corrie was the beneficiary of Duffy's sage advice. She listened well. He would've been proud.

Faith was born and raised in Honolulu, Hawaii. She and her husband, Bernard, moved to San Diego, California, in 1984. Corrie and Faith found the world of canine sports together and competed in agility and obedience since 2006. A new puppy is on the way in 2014.

Acknowledgments

Miracles happen when one life touches another. It can change the course of that person's journey. My path changed when I met my life and business coach, Dezi Koster. She asked me what I was passionate about, and I told her I *love* dogs but didn't see how a pastime could evolve into a business. During the conversation, I blurted out that I'd thought about writing a book "someday." She replied, "The time is *now*!" With that said, she guided a reticent novice toward a finished manuscript in seven months.

A week after I finished my draft, Terry Whalin of Morgan James Publishing hosted a webinar about writing a book proposal and finding a champion. I had no idea how he came my way, but I realized, after speaking to him a few minutes, I'd found my champion. His kindness and nurturing brought me to Author 101 University's Writers Conference, where I met Rick Frishman and his wonderful wife, Bobbi. Rick liked my book concept and encouraged me to submit my proposal. The rest, as they say, is history.

To David Hancock and his wonderful publishing team, I cannot thank you enough for making my dream a reality. To Amanda Rooker and her editing team, your expertise and honest feedback helped me dig deeper to make this book better than I thought possible.

Two friends, Alyssa Freas and Pete Peterson, helped me believe in myself and my book. Alyssa reminds me that gratitude and caring is a lifelong habit. I met Pete at a writer's group gathering. He gave me several hours of his time over a couple of months, mentoring and encouraging me with my book. He gave me a quote that I will never forget: "What you are looking for is looking for you." I carry this in my heart because with each occurrence that pushes me closer to my dream, I see how insightful he is.

I owe a lot to all my dog owner friends. There are too many to name but a few I want to thank. Ronni Russell is my agility mentor and role model. We first met in an agility class. She guided and supported me from our very first competition. She's been there ever since, through all our good times and bad. She never coddled me or minced words, but she was always, first and foremost, my friend. Dayle and Ron Moden gave me the best little girl in Corrie. She always aimed to please. Watching her grow and excel in all the activities I'd wished we could've experienced with Duffy were the happiest moments of my life.

Bernard, my husband, endured persistent allergy attacks, injuries, and late-night cleanups because he knew my life was incomplete without a dog. Very few people would tolerate the years of personal hardship and sacrifice he suffered with Duffy. His patience and support gave an otherwise throwaway dog a forever home. I will always love him and be indebted to him for making this possible.

So, in keeping with one life touching another to change that person's journey, Duffy certainly changed mine. He also created a legacy and opened my eyes to so many new adventures for the little sister he left behind.

I hope you enjoyed experiencing this journey with us. Duffy would like to give you a free gift to thank you for your purchase of this book.

Please go to

www.duffysworldthebook.com/gift

to make your selection.
We hope to see you at the movie soon!